TWAYNE'S WORLD AUTHORS SERIES
A Survey of the World's Literature

AUSTRALIA

Joseph Jones, University of Texas

EDITOR

Xavier Herbert

TWAS 552

Xavier Herbert

XAVIER HERBERT

By LAURIE CLANCY
La Trobe University

TWAYNE PUBLISHERS

A DIVISION OF G. K. HALL & CO., BOSTON

Copyright © 1981 by G. K. Hall & Co.

Published in 1981 by Twayne Publishers,
A Division of G. K. Hall & Co.
All Rights Reserved

Printed on permanent/durable acid-free paper and bound
in the United States of America

First Printing

Library of Congress Cataloging in Publication Data
Clancy, Laurie, 1942-
Xavier Herbert.
(Twayne's world authors series ; TWAS 552 : Australia)
Bibliography: p. 143-46
Includes index.
1. Herbert, Xavier, 1901-   —Criticism and interpretation.
PR9619.3.H38Z62 1981   823   80-27487
ISBN 0-8057-6394-5

To my friend and colleague
Jenny Wightman

Contents

About the Author

Laurie Clancy was born in Melbourne, Australia, in 1942, and was educated by the Christian Brothers and then at the University of Melbourne, from which he graduated in 1964 with an Honours degree in English and History. He taught in the English department at Melbourne before moving to the newly formed La Trobe University in 1967, where he still teaches, as Senior Lecturer.

In 1969 Mr. Clancy visited the United States of America for the first time on a two year Harkness Fellowship, and has since returned there several times. In 1973 he completed his Master of Arts thesis on the fiction of Vladimir Nabokov for which he was awarded first-class honours; a revised version of this will be published by MacMillan's in London.

In 1975 he published his first novel, *A Collapsible Man*, which shared the National Book Award for fiction and which was later released in the United States by St. Martin's Press. His first collection of short stories, *The Wife Specialist*, was published in 1980.

Mr. Clancy's short stories and articles have been published in most leading Australian newspapers and literary journals and he now divides his writing time equally between fiction and literary and cultural criticism. He is also a member of the editorial board of the Australian short story journal, *Tabloid Story*. He has recently published a monograph on the Australian novelist Christina Stead and his second novel, *Masters*, has been submitted to a publisher.

Preface

Xavier Herbert, a writer probably known to most Australians, probably is to an equal extent unknown outside his native land. Of the three living really distinguished Australian novelists as of the time of this writing—Patrick White, Christina Stead and Herbert—the first two are as well known overseas as they are in Australia. White, who in any case was born in England, returned to settle in Australia only when almost into middle age. Christina Stead, who left her homeland for England when only a young woman, for most of her life lived there, in the United States and in various parts of Europe. She returned to live in Australia only a few years ago, at the age of nearly seventy. White's work is deeply and unselfconsciously cosmopolitan in nature, easily accessible to nonAustralians, even though most of it from *The Tree of Man* onwards is set here. Christina Stead is even more obviously an international writer, the citizen of no particular country in her fiction. Only one complete novel—*Seven Poor Men of Sydney*—and about half of another—*For Love Alone*—are set in Australia and the notion of a consciously held national identity is totally alien to her. For her best, and best known novel, the avowedly autobiographical *The Man Who Loved Children*, she transferred the whole setting, lock, stock, and barrel, from Sydney, Australia to Baltimore, Maryland.

I Herbert's Nationalism

Unlike Patrick White and Christina Stead, Herbert is, on the other hand, a totally and admittedly nationalistic and—in the oldfashioned, literal sense of the word—chauvinistic Australian. He has been overseas—to England—only once and on his return vowed never to leave his native land again, a promise he has faithfully kept. He once described his first novel *Capricornia* as "A hymn-book in adoration of Australia"[1] and although his attitudes towards his fellow countrymen have become a good deal more ambivalent since then—his latest novel *Poor Fellow My Country* could be fairly described as a dirge in lament of the Australia that might have been—there is no doubt that he has remained thoroughly and pervasively Australian throughout his life and work.

Herbert is ruthlessly honest about this parochial element in his work and its effect on the degree to which he could ever become internationally recognized. In 1963 he told an interviewer:

> You have got to realize that an Australian writer or any writer belonging to a small country must be satisfied with the success in his own country. The reason why Patrick White and Morris West are successful overseas is that they write about things objectively and they write about other countries.
>
> My first book, 'Capricornia', had an essentially Australian quality. The people overseas go for it because it is a sort of denunciation of Australia. The English were very shocked because they always thought Australia was a decent, clean country. 'Capricornia' is always popular behind the Iron Curtain because it is useful propaganda. It has kept us over the years, bought our home, fed us.
>
> Even so I've never sold a short story overseas and I've tried often.[2]

There are elements in this statement that are highly questionable, such as the sufficiency of its account of Patrick White's international success, as well as the coupling of his name with that of Morris West. Nevertheless, it remains a striking phenomenon that this prophet is acclaimed in his own country but scarcely anywhere else. If his novels sell in England they certainly receive no critical attention there and it will be interesting to see whether the huge commercial success of his latest novel *Poor Fellow My Country* will do anything to change that situation overseas. Herbert's relative obscurity as a writer overseas, as well as qualities indigenous to his work, make him a difficult figure to introduce to international—and especially American—audiences.

Moreover, there is a more specific quality in Herbert's nationalism which helps to make access to his writing often difficult. His Australia is not the contemporary Australia of some fourteen million people mostly gathered together in five cities ("five cities, like five teeming sores,/Each drains her," in the words of one of our leading poets[3])—a country highly urbanized, highly motorized, highly materialistic, with a vast, barren outback that Australians boast about to visitors but rarely go and see for themselves. Herbert's Australia is of an older and rarer vintage. The best account of it he gives himself in a letter to a friend written in the nineteen thirties:

> Now I shall tell you about myself. I was born and reared in the bush. I love the bush. The spirit of the Land is my diety (*sic*). I had contact with

Aborigines from my earliest days. They were never peculiar and outlandish creatures to me, but part of the scheme of things, men and women to be considered like all others, and more, to be respected because of their closer communion with my diety.

Even during my early education in a civilized place I was in close contact with the bush. I remember my years from sixteen to twenty-one as a succession of dawns; for it was my habit to rise always before daylight and watch the dawn spread over the bush. Not till I came to the Eastern States at the age of twenty-two had I ever slept in a place out of sight of the bush. The bush is my home. Blue vistas hold no mystery for me. I know what they contain. I view them with much the same feeling as I would my homestead when viewing from afar . . .

I spent three years in the cities of the Eastern States. I was never comfortable. Glimpses of blue vistas always made my heart ache. It was during those years that I learnt to be cynical. I had imagined that all Australians were as close to understanding of the soil from which they sprang as I. Thus my countrymen of Western Australia had seemed, and hence one could forgive their ignorance of other matters. I wished to write. I did not dabble in ordinary accepted kinds of writing long, for soon it dawned on me that the most outstanding subject in the land was the ignorance of the Land by the people living in it. Then I went North to the Territory, knowing that I should find there the Spirit of the Land much as it had always been, and find it in the keeping of its own children the Aborigines. My love of the land and trust in it were proved by the fact that I made my journey by simply heading into the wilderness and going whither distant hills and stars might lead me. That was ten years ago.

I went to commune with the Spirit of the Land, but found something much more urgent to give my attention to—the unutterable misery of its custodians. Since then the cause of the Aborigines has dominated my life. Perhaps unfortunately, I sought to present their case through literature. Being by nature painstaking, I was forced to subdue much of my feeling in the matter so as not to interfere with my art. I struggled in this literary phrase 'till about eighteen months ago, when, despairing of ever being able to do what I wished with words, I decided to apply myself to deeds, and therefore returned to this country, again using the stars and hills to guide me through the wilderness. Since my return I have devoted myself to the cause of the Aborigines, and in a matter of months have done far more even in understanding them myself than previously I had done in years.[4]

This moving and highly revealing description of the author's feelings for his native land and the people from whom it was taken is worth looking at for several reasons. Particularly noteworthy is Herbert's very real and intense feeling, rare in an Australian white man, for the Australian Aborigines. This is not the place to discuss the attitude of white Australians towards people of other races except to say that if racial prejudice is, as I believe it is, endemic to white peoples, then Australians are certainly no exception. The main difference, perhaps, between the American historical experience and ours is that the first settlers of Australia encountered far less militant resistance from the blacks in the appropriation of their land and consequently wiped them out far more thoroughly than the Americans vis-à-vis the Indians. In the island of Tasmania, for instance, not a single fullblooded black person was left alive by 1885, out of an estimated original population of four to five thousand. The opening of *Capricornia* itself documents the simple strategems (offering them gifts of poisoned flour, for example) by which the blacks' generosity and trustfulness were taken advantage of.

However, Xavier Herbert is one exception. As he says, he was brought up largely among blacks in Western Australia. His autobiography *Disturbing Element* recounts, for example, the half-comic, half-poignant incident of a black prostitute whom he had known slightly as a child many years before who helps him to overcome his continuing revulsion towards sexuality and initiates him into sexual experience. He had continually struggled to bring the Aborigines' plight to the attention of the white authorities (usually, it must be admitted, through no fault of his own, without success) and worked for a time as Aboriginal Protector of the compound in Darwin, Northern Territory.

Much of his writing, then, is prompted by a deep feeling of rage at the treatment of Aborigines in Australia. When *Capricornia* appeared in 1938 it was understandably interpreted as a propagandistic work exposing the inhumane treatment of Aborigines, especially of the half-castes in the Northern Territory. A London reviewer wrote, for instance, that "Mr. Herbert's study of the half-caste problem is fearless, and he is to be congratulated on his courage in stating the truth as he sees it. The social historian of Australia in years to come will find it invaluable." Furnley Maurice in the *Australian Quarterly* wrote that the novel is "Written with ruthless courage . . . packed with substance . . . . And there is the steady recurrence of the sinister 'black velvet' theme, knock, knock, knock in your brain like the tom-toms in the jungle that followed Emperor Jones."[5] Most other contemporary reviewers, though they failed to catch Maurice's tom-toms, reacted in generally similar terms.

It was not until the publication of a brilliant, and highly influential study of the novel by Professor Vincent Buckley of the University of Melbourne in 1960[6] that attention was drawn to the formally innovative and radical elements in the novel, unique in Australian fiction up until then, and that the book came to be seen as more than an example of racy, essentially propagandistic naturalism. Although I believe Professor Buckley's approach is the most valuable one, as I argue later in the chapter devoted to *Capricornia*, I think also that there is a danger of the critical pendulum swinging too far the other way, with the element of social realism and protest in the novel being played down. Whatever its aesthetically innovative qualities, conscious or unconscious, the source of the novel's power, at least initially, is in its author's indignation at the treatment of the blacks and his compassion for their predicament. Despite the unconvincing idealization of the black character Prindy in *Poor Fellow My Country* Herbert's writing is at its best, both in that novel and in *Capricornia*, when he is dealing with the black people and with the geographical areas where they live, since he himself knows these best.

The second point to note about the already quoted extract from the letter is that Herbert repeatedly states his preference for the bush over the city. One of the classic Australian dichotomies is expressed in the idiomatic phrase "Sydney or the Bush" and Herbert has made his choice abundantly clear over and over again. Just as he writes best about black people and the land they live in, so also does much of his worst writing—in *Soldiers' Women*, for instance, with its setting of urban Sydney, and in the urban sections of *Poor Fellow My Country*—arise out of his descriptions of the large Australian cities, from which he draws back with horror, regarding them as depersonalized, anonymous jungles. Herbert is a regional writer, not only by virtue of the fact that he is an Australian writing on indigenously Australian themes and often characters but also for his major writing being mostly devoted to a particular and little known area of Australia, the country in the far North to which he has given the mythical name of Capricornia (much as William Faulkner dramatized and documented Yoknapatawpha County).

In response to a questionnaire from an academic scholar, Dr. J. B. Beston, concerned with fellow writer Hal Porter, Herbert wrote in 1972: "I feel that privily he would subscribe to the coterie that says that *I myself* ('Orrible 'Erbie) am the worst thing that ever happened to Australian Literature, because I've kept it behind 'The

Slip-Rails', just when it was ready to get out."[7] I have no idea what Porter would say to such an imputation, but the truth is very much the reverse. The great triumph of *Capricornia* is that it is both a thoroughly Australian novel—one which could have come out of no other society or culture—and at the same time a novel of universal appeal and range. It deserves far greater attention than it has so far enjoyed, and that consideration itself is a justification for this study.

II   *Herbert's Achievement*

The plan of the book is simple. In Chapter Two I have attempted a brief biographical account of the author, as well as providing for readers who are likely to be unfamiliar with it, some introduction to the social context in which he writes. The task has not been easy, especially as Herbert himself very courteously declined either to be interviewed or to answer queries by mail. The main source of information is Herbert's engaging and impressively honest autobiography *Disturbing Element;* but this takes his story up only to the age of twenty-four. For the rest of Herbert's long life (he was born in 1901—one year before Christina Stead, and eleven before Patrick White) I have had to rely on a number of autobiographical articles he has published irregularly over the years and interviews he has granted, but there are necessarily many gaps. In addition, there are a number of fascinating letters by the author stored in the National Library in Canberra (the most revealing are those such as the one quoted from earlier, written in the nineteen thirties, after the writing of *Capricornia* but before its publication, to his wife Sadie and friend Arthur Dibley), on which I have drawn. They reveal him as almost surprisingly aware of what he is doing in his fiction, pragmatic in his approach to it, generous with his friends and also highly introspective for a man with such a reputation for gregariousness and aggressive public behavior.

Herbert has, in all, published six books: *Capricornia* (1938), *Seven Emus* (1959), *Soldiers' Women* (1961), *Disturbing Element* (1963), *Larger Than Life* (1963), and *Poor Fellow My Country* (1975). There also exist a number of uncollected short stories, and other prose pieces, as well as numerous references throughout his life to incomplete, abandoned, or even rejected projects. For instance, Herbert reportedly wrote an entire long novel in the early nineteen forties, *Yeller Feller*, which he later burned, because it was too like *Capricornia*.

Seven Emus is a minor, not very distinguished novel, written primarily to demonstrate the efficacy of a somewhat eccentric mode of punctuation which Herbert himself devised (in this it was a signal failure). *Disturbing Element* has been mentioned as one of his most attractive books. *Larger Than Life* is a selected gathering from the stories Herbert wrote in the early nineteen thirties, when he was struggling to live as a professional writer. They are conventional in form but well-crafted pieces (an account given in Herbert's letters of how they came to be written is discussed later) and both this book and *Disturbing Element* are welcome additions to his total *oeuvre*. Nevertheless, I am sure that the author himself would agree that it is on his three major novels that any definitive assessment of his achievement as a writer must be based. Therefore although this study devotes a chapter to each of the six works (in chronological order except for the biographical Chapter Two which discusses *Disturbing Element*), it is on *Capricornia, Soldiers' Women,* and *Poor Fellow My Country* that its attention is chiefly focussed.

"Any fool," Herbert is quoted as saying, "can write one good book. It takes a good man to write two good books."[8] I believe Herbert is wrong and that it is given to very few of us indeed to write even one book as good as *Capricornia*. But if he is to be taken at his word, then it is the contention of this study that Herbert has failed to satisfy his own criterion and that the other two novels of major ambition are, relatively speaking, artistic failures.

When it first appeared, *Capricornia* was received with enormous critical enthusiasm. Even now it is the only work of Herbert's to have received detailed critical attention, and its place in Australian literature seems assured. Commercially it did not do so well at first, partly owing to the peculiar circumstances of its publication, to be discussed later in Chapter Three. Herbert told Patricia Rolfe in an interview that it was published in an edition of two thousand and that "Angus and Robertson, of course, blackballed it. But Anthony Horderns—are they still going?—bought up the remainder and I went in myself at Christmas and sold it."[9] Later, it won the Commonwealth sesquicentenary prize and the Australian Literature Society's gold medal and was later published in England, the United States of America and many other countries. It has since run through many editions, and to leave it off a course in Australian literature would be like leaving *Moby Dick* off an American literature course.

Soldiers' Women which appeared in 1961, however, was almost universally panned by the critics. There were a few exceptions, such as the novelist Gavin Casey, but a more representative judgment would be that of Geoffrey Dutton, who wrote: "The theme is worthy of the author of *Capricornia*, with its huge possibilities of tragedy and comedy; likewise the book itself is big enough, and has had enough time and work spent on it, to be a major novel. It is not. It is an appalling and embarrassing flop."[10]

However, the book still sells, perhaps partly owing to the sensational nature of its subject matter—women, freed of their marital commitments, on the loose in wartime Sydney—and Herbert has told Patricia Rolfe that the book, which his English publishers keep constantly in print has been his means of livelihood since it was published (it will be recalled that earlier in this chapter he was quoted as saying much the same thing about *Capricornia*).

The publication of *Poor Fellow My Country* revived interest in Herbert's work among critics as well as the general public; already a number of articles have appeared for and against the novel. When the novel first appeared it was to generally laudatory reviews, although some were ambiguous in tone. Brian Kiernan in *The Age* in Melbourne, for example, wrote a carefully expository, neutral review, concluding with the cautious and self-evident words ". . . regretfully though it is not another *Capricornia*."[11] Only *Overland* magazine published a highly critical and reasonably extensive review article by Edward Kynaston[12] and in the following issue a longer, equally unflattering article by Don Grant.[13] And even then the editor of the periodical, Dr. Stephen Murray-Smith, felt obliged to print an apologetic note, insisting that he had no desire to victimize Herbert. These articles provoked a reply from Laurie Hergenhan in a further issue of *Overland*[14] and in addition Geoffrey Dutton, who dismissed *Soldiers' Women* out of hand in his review of the novel when it first appeared, has since declared Herbert's latest novel a "work of genius."[15]

I have no doubt that *Poor Fellow My Country* will continue to provoke far more critical discussion and dissension than *Soldiers' Women*, if only because of its extraordinary length (eight hundred and fifty-thousand words, or one third longer than *War and Peace*) and equally extraordinary commercial success. Within eighteen months of publication the novel had gone into a third hardback printing, totalling twenty-eight thousand copies, and the price had risen from twenty Australian dollars to twenty-eight dollars. (Publication of the book was made possible in the first place only by a government subsidy.) The paperback version sold similarly well, and its success has fortunately allowed Herbert's earlier works to be reissued in paperback. Of course, it is impossible to tell how much of the book's popularity is owing to skilful promotion on the part of its English publishers, William Collins, or how many people who bought the book actually read it right through to the end. (I know of at least two critics who reviewed it in daily newspapers without finishing it, but on the other hand some people who scarcely or never read a book have read right through it with pleasure.) In any case, that its acceptance is substantial and widespread has been confirmed by its winning the prestigious Miles Franklin Award for the best Australian work of fiction published in 1975.

My own view is, as I suggested, that the work is an artistic failure of a rather catastrophic kind, that it rates with Frank Dalby Davidson's *The White Thorntree*, another fictional leviathan, as the two novels in Australian history in which ambition and accomplishment are most conspicuously at odds with one another. I have tried to explain as sympathetically but impartially as I can why I think so in the chapter devoted to the novel. If that view is correct, then the literary career of Xavier Herbert assumes a curious perspective, that of a man whose first published novel became a great Australian classic and who has struggled for forty years afterwards, mostly in isolation, and with heroic artistic integrity but without success, to repeat his achievement. If it is accepted, also, it will probably revive the age old controversy of P. R. Stephensen's claims to have substantially cut and "edited" *Capricornia* (see Chapter Two). Herbert, who insisted on publishing *Poor Fellow My Country* exactly as it was, without cuts or changes, was encouraged in this by two academic critics, Dr. Harry Heseltine of James Cook University and Dr. Laurie Hergenhan of the University of Queensland, who have consistently and bravely championed the cause of Herbert's writing.

III *Criticism of Herbert's Writing*

As I mentioned earlier, with the exception of *Capricornia*, criticism of Herbert's fiction is virtually nonexistent, except for journalistic reviews too short to make much contribution which appeared at the time of each work's first publication. The only extended study is Dr. Heseltine's contribution to the Oxford University Press series on Australian writers and their work. Although for reasons I discuss later on I disagree with many of Heseltine's conclusions, his is a stimulating and valuable argument. The bibliography at the end of this book largely follows that of Heseltine's, with the addition of new contributions that have appeared since 1973. I have included ephemeral pieces, such as newspaper reviews, only when they seemed to throw a particular light on the novels. The bibliography, complete up until December, 1977, tries as far as possible to encompass work done on Herbert since then that has come to my attention. However, I had no opportunity to take advantage of the very thorough and exhaustive checklist of Xavier Herbert's writings, compiled by Marianne Ehrhardt and Lurline Stuart, which appeared in *Australian Literary Studies*, Volume Eight, number four, just as this volume was going to press.

LAURIE CLANCY

La Trobe University
Bundoora, Victoria, Australia

Acknowledgments

I should like to thank the following people who have assisted me in writing this book in one way or another: Clem Christesen, foundation editor of *Meanjin Quarterly*, who first suggested that I should do it, and Professor Joseph Jones, of the University of Texas, who agreed, and who proved subsequently most patient and helpful; John Barnes and Jenny Wightman, of the Department of English at La Trobe, who read the manuscript and made many useful suggestions; Miriam Grosvenor, who proved most helpful with research and with her pithy comments on the critical articles consulted; Sue Dwyer, Anne Miles and Julie Orlowski, who typed the manuscript impeccably; and finally, of course, my wife Kate who was an enormous source of encouragement and assistance.

L. C.

Chronology

1901   Xavier Herbert born in the town of Port Hedland, on the Northwest coast of Western Australia.

1913   The family moves south to Fremantle, W.A.

1915   Herbert's half-brother Phillip leaves to fight overseas. Herbert is fired from his job after a row about seeing him off. He enrolls in a Christian Brothers College.

1918   Herbert passes the Preliminary Pharmaceutical examination. Goes to work as a pharmaceutical apprentice.

1921   Herbert qualifies as a pharmacist.

1923   Herbert travels to Melbourne to study medicine.

1925   Herbert leaves Melbourne for Sydney and gives up both medical and pharmaceutical careers. His first stories are published around this time.

1930   Herbert sails from Darwin to London, en route writing unpublished novel *Black Velvet*.

1931 (circa)   Herbert meets Sadie Norden, who encourages him in his writing. Two years later, after he has returned to Australia, she follows and marries him.

1932   *Capricornia* completed. Rejected by an English publisher. Herbert returns home.

1933   Herbert meets P. R. Stephensen, also returned from England and now running the Endeavour Press. He accepts *Capricornia* for publication but while the novel is being set up in type the firm goes bankrupt. Herbert lives as a writer, doing short stories and pieces for *Smith's Weekly*.

1935-1936   Herbert works as acting Superintendent of the Aboriginals in Darwin, Northern Territory. Attempts to secure the position for him on a permanent basis fail.

1937   February, *Capricornia* again accepted by Stephensen, who is now running the Publicist Press.

1937   December 31, Stephensen prints and binds one copy of the novel and submits it, just in time, for the Commonwealth Sesquicentenary Literary Competition.

1938   March 31, *Capricornia* wins the novel section of the competition, value £250. Angus & Robertson take up the rights to the novel and reprint it.

1940   Herbert wins the Gold Medal of the Australian Literary Society. He receives a Commonwealth Literary Fund award, valued at £250.

1942- Herbert serves in the Australian army in the Pacific cam-
1944   paign, rising to the rank of sergeant.

1946   Discharged, he and Sadie settle at Redlynch in Northern Queensland.

1952   Herbert is awarded a Commonwealth Literary Fund half fellowship, value £300. During the 1950s he learns to fly aircraft.

1957   Herbert is awarded a full Commonwealth Literary Fund grant, value £1000.

1959   Publication of *Seven Emus*.

1960   *Meanjin*, devoting part of a special issue to his work, includes an extract from a novel in progress, *I, The Little Widow, & The World*, which was never published.

1961   *Soldiers' Women* published.

1961   March, Herbert quarrels with Stephensen in the pages of *The Bulletin* over how *Capricornia* came to be edited and published.

1963   *Disturbing Element* and *Larger Than Life* published.

1975   *Poor Fellow My Country* published and becomes an immediate best seller.

1976   Herbert awarded the Miles Franklin Literary Award for the best novel of the year.

CHAPTER 1

Biography

A LFRED Francis Xavier Herbert was born in Port Hedland, a
tiny seaport on the Northwest coast of Western Australia, in
1901, the year in which Australia achieved federation. His father
was a Welshman and a railway engine driver, which helps to explain
the continual fascination Herbert displays in *Capricornia* for trains.
His mother, of mixed English and Irish stock, apparently thought
England and Scotland were the only two countries worth being
proud of. She despised the nationality of both her husband and son.

In an "Autobiographette" which appeared in *The Publicist* in
1938 Herbert wrote:

> The first experience of my life recorded in my memory is that of toddling
> (I was only a baby at the time) along a sun-silvered strip of sand on which
> broke the sparkling ripples of the Indian Ocean: the next is that of running
> naked over hard red grassless ground in a rain-storm, with my tongue stuck
> out to catch the drops, the scene of this experience doubtless being some
> mining-camp in the vast red wilderness that lies behind the shores of the
> locality in which I was born.[1]

According to the account offered in *Disturbing Element*, Herbert's mother Victoria left the nursing of him to her black servants.
Soon after birth he contracted a severe gastric disease and for the
first twelve months of his life appeared highly unlikely to survive.
He did so, however, and became as he says "the healthiest of kids"[2]
(although he always felt that in comparison to his half-brother
Philip—his mother having had two children by an earlier
marriage—his position in the family was a rather ambiguous and
often peripheral one).

I   *The Disturbing Element*

Whatever its factual accuracy almost every one of the themes and
preoccupations that appear in Herbert's fiction can be found in
embryonic form in the account the author offers of his early life in

Disturbing Element. The love of railways, the youthful preoccupation with playing soldiers with his brother that later surfaces in the figure of Tim O'Cannon in *Capricornia*, the unselfconscious respect for the Aborigines with whom he lived on intimate terms, his fascination with the beauty of the Australian landscape, his emerging nationalism—all these are already present. In the "Autobiographette" he mentions the inscription on the wall of the little weatherboard-and-iron State School that reads: "The empire is my country—Australia is my home"; and the theme of loss or confusion of identity—national, cultural, familial—recurs constantly through the book, as it will later in the fiction. Like the figure of The Shouter in *Capricornia*, Herbert's own father lived in contempt of most other men but was thoroughly intimidated by his wife. We find in this account the same derision of Australians for the ease with which they could be inveigled into fighting English imperialist wars that is found in both *Capricornia* and *Poor Fellow My Country.* There is here also the same criticism of the Irish in Fremantle, Western Australia (on the grounds of their sentimentality) that will later appear in *Poor Fellow My Country,* although there in a much more bitter and less genial form.

There are even names in the autobiography which are repeated later in the fiction. His mother claimed apocryphal ancestors on the French side with the name de Lacey—almost identical to the name of the hero in *Poor Fellow My Country.* Billy Bray, the bottle-oh (or collector of empty bottles for profit) is obviously the ancestor of Billy Brew in the same novel. The title of a chapter in the autobiography, "Dawn of a New Era," is again found in *Capricornia,* while even the title of the autobiography—the irritated description Herbert's father used to offer him—is found in that novel as well.

But without doubt the most important question of identity has to do with Herbert's relationship with his parents, especially his father, and his need to justify himself in their eyes. His feelings were complicated firstly by what he saw as his mother's domination over his father and secondly, his sense that he himself was an unwanted intruder (a "disturbing element") into what had been an almost Edenic situation. Of those early years he writes:

So I conclude that I was unwanted when I entered that early happy household which comprised my parents, my noble grandfather, and those children whose existence up to date had not been so felicitous as to make them eager to share the new condition with a brat who appeared out of the blue. However, strangers remain unwelcome only by being unpleasant. I am ready to admit that it was as much my fault as my family's, and even more, that I never got along with them, for all that I mostly truckled to them. The very inconsistency of mostly truckling and then of blazing into indignation when my humility was too grossly taken advantage of was surely cause for misunderstanding and strife.[3]

In particular, he speaks almost constantly of his fear of his father and of his sense of faiure in his attempts to satisfy his father's expectations. As Harry Heseltine has shown, it is a recurrent theme in his fiction as well as in his autobiographical writings. "Apart from convincing myself that my father was my enemy," he writes in *Disturbing Element,* "I have been preoccupied for most of my life with trying to overcome the cowardice I believed due to his malicious mishandling of me."[4] In true Freudian fashion (though elsewhere he is sceptical of Freud) Herbert speaks of "the primal spiritual struggle of the human male" as "adjustment to animal rivalry between the son and the father whom eventually the son must supersede for the advancement of the species."[5] A whole chapter of the book is devoted to a painful account of the author's attempts—and failure—to become a skilful horseman like his father and half-brother Philip, and to the feeling of psychological inferiority the struggle left him with.

It is a preoccupation that was never to leave him. Much later, in 1964, he published a closely autobiographical piece entitled "My Thousandth Death" in which he recalled the first thirty years of his life which he spent partly trying to ride horses—"Then and there a man's manhood was largely measured by his horsemanship"[6]—and explains how he finally overcame his sense of inferiority by learning how to fly an aircraft when he was in his mid-fifties.

II   *Adolescence*

When Herbert was twelve the family moved South to Fremantle. His mother had had two more children in the meantime, Victoria and Horatio; but when both died in infancy from illness, Xavier remained the solitary boy he describes himself as being throughout his early days. Later there was another child, Bill. After the move Herbert went at first to a fairly large State boys' school.

According to his own evidence he was a very poor student who suffered under the tutelage of a tyrannical schoolmaster. It may be

noted parenthetically here that *Disturbing Element* is not to be
completely trusted as a factual account. There are blatant contradic-
tions between the events recounted there and those in earlier
autobiographical pieces Herbert wrote, when presumably his memory was fresher and when perhaps he did not feel the need, as he
puts it in the opening words of *Disturbing Element*, "To avoid the
heart-burning that may otherwise be caused by so frank a history as
I intend this to be."[7] For instance, in *Disturbing Element* the first
teacher Herbert meets is the calm, wise Miss Guillain, "the first
woman for whom I truly felt love."[8] In the "Autobiographette" she
is merely "a raw-boned English spinster."[9] Similarly, it is she who
runs the classroom in which the words "THE EMPIRE IS MY
COUNTRY—AUSTRALIA IS MY HOME" may be found. In
Disturbing Element the adjective BRITISH has been added, the
inscription is now in the room of the hated teacher Mr. Grassapple,
and it is he who harangues the unfortunate pupils about their
glorious British heritage. At any rate, if his account of his scholastic
ability is to be accepted, the only subjects at which he showed talent
were Chemistry (earlier he had experimented with a number of
chemical substances found in an abandoned hospital), and what was
then known as English Composition, at which he received very little
encouragement.

He learned far more in those days, as since, outside the classroom
in the company of an older boy named Bushy Bushby (the names in
Disturbing Element are as apocryphal as some of the events) with
whom he roamed all over the town of Fremantle, exploring the
ships, the cemetery, the Corn Barn where the trams were housed
and having his older friend point out the madhouse and the
brothels.

In *Disturbing Element* Herbert describes an incident and its
aftermath which clearly had an enormous effect on him in later life
and especially on the ideas about sexuality he espouses in *Poor
Fellow My Country*. One day he sailed a tiny boat out to a wreck.
He was playing there, hanging by his hands from a beam, when two
beautiful young girls emerged naked from the water and proceeded
to dry themselves. Unseen by them he hung painfully on—determined that their idyll would not be ruined by discovery of an
intruder—until they had gone.

The incident is significant in two respects. Herbert's discovery of
his own sexual passions seems to have been followed by an acute

insight into those of his father, and of his father's forced repression of them. He speaks of himself as "having come to realize, by the time I was entangled in my helplessness, that he was as helpless as I, was doing much the same thing with his strength as I, only the medium of his emasculation was no succubus of fantasy, but a flesh and blood harpy in his bed."[10]

Secondly emerged the belief, to be reiterated many times, that sexual activity was an expenditure and loss of self, a loss of creative potency: that its potentially explosive energy could be sublimated and harnessed to some other cause—to fictive expression, for instance. "If only," he laments, "I'd had someone, some hero, some knight, to guide me then, to show me how to conserve that power from my genitals and win with it the treasure it offers, sublimated, in exaltation of the spirit."[11] Shortly after this, he completed his first piece of writing, a story called "The Speaking Fish," "the burden of which," he says, "is sublimation of sexual desire."[12] So firmly does Herbert hold to these ideas that he has been known to go into total solitude while working on his writing. As he put it:

I used to stay writing in my camp, in complete isolation, for twenty-one days at a time. Then I would go down to Sadie at Redlynch for rations and a day or two of talking with my kind—never for anything else, though: for celibacy was the mainstay of the state of saintly ecstacy I had acquired. Sweet Sadie, fearing that continence was driving me nuts, was ever ready to do the Delilah on me.[13]

There remains one more sexual incident worth recounting from this period, if only because, although Herbert dismisses it in only half a page in *Disturbing Element* he gives a very much fuller account of a similar incident in a semiautobiographical piece entitled "I, the Little Widow, and the World," published in *Meanjin Quarterly* in 1960 as part of a projected book which was never completed.[14] The story concerns an incident the narrator hears on returning to a Queensland town after a solitary trek in the bush. A young man, believed by the town to be a semi-imbecile, is arrested for molesting a little girl, and in his shame, he has hanged himself in jail. The narrator is filled with a double sense of guilt: at his recollection of having failed to help the young man embark on the career he thought he could have managed successfully many years before, but also for having indulged in a similar and half-conscious "crime" many years before, but having been treated very much more understandingly by the child's kindhearted and sensible mother. The account of this original incident is virtually identical to that given in *Disturbing Element.*

The episode is significant, not only for the unflinching self-honesty with which Herbert confronts it in his memory but also because it epitomizes one of the central elements in Herbert's vision of human existence. In Christian terms, it is "There but for the grace of God go I." In pagan terms, it is a recognition, so central to *Capricornia,* of the element of the contingent, the accidental, in deciding a human being's fate. The narrator is helped by a sensible woman; Lennie Kingborn, confronted with total lack of sympathy or understanding in a similar situation, is driven to suicide, just as Ducky Drake in *Disturbing Element,* "the electrical genius and son of a burglar"[15] is hounded to his death in similar circumstances by a community which judges him solely by his father's example.

Shortly before World War I broke out, Herbert's father, increasingly tense under the strain of an unhappy marriage to a woman who seemed to have little respect for him, arranged a kind of semipermanent separation by travelling to England. When war was declared, however, instead of enlisting as his brother Merlin urged, he returned to Western Australia to make arrangements for the family. In 1915 Xavier himself suffered the humiliation—one of a seemingly endless series at this time—of being rejected for service as a Naval Cadet and hence having his fears about his own lack of masculinity confirmed yet again.

At the age of fourteen Herbert left school and immediately found a job working for a pharmacist, in this way following up his passion for chemistry. At the same time he attended night school three times a week. This triumph, however, proved to be short lived. The pharmacist made life a misery for him, as most of his teachers had done, with constant verbal abuse, accusations of onanism, and stories he spread about him to the other adolescents in the district, so that he became a publically vilified figure. At last, however, the tormented boy was able to assert himself. He gained the respect of the local boys by standing up to the most renowned fighter in the district and refusing to be defeated by him. Then, after his pharmacist refused to grant him leave to see his half-brother Phil off to war Herbert defied him and when the man fired him gave him a verbal lashing. He returned home, fearful of his mother's reaction to his getting the sack, to find that his father had been called up for service and that she was actually glad to have him at home more often. He returned to fulltime school, this time at the Christian Brothers' College, to study for the Preliminary Pharmaceutical exam.

III *Early Manhood*

Herbert mentions early in his autobiography that though the family were baptized Catholics, they rejected the authority of the Church, as they did the authority of almost every other institutiton. One day a critic or psychoanalyst will attempt to answer the question why so many Australian writers, especially writers of fiction, had an Irish-Catholic upbringing, and why so many of them wrote novels in which they excoriated it. In contrast to most others, however, Herbert seems to have flourished under the upbringing, and through the influence of a certain Brother Ignatius, whom he describes as being "nearer to being a saint than anyone I've ever dealt with"[16] he came closer to a religious frame of mind than at any other time of his life.

At the same time as this was going on, however, Herbert was also experiencing the first of many love affairs—mostly unhappy, unconsummated, and often conducted at some distance from the beloved—which occupy the later pages of *Disturbing Element*. One was with Theresa, the daughter of an Austrian businessman interned at the time, and another with Huldah, a German Jewess. Herbert's frequently expressed admiration for the Jewish race thus seems to have preceded his meeting with his future wife Sadie whom, rather surprisingly given his mother's other bigotries, she encouraged him to woo.

The culmination of these experiences came on Armistice Day, 1918, when Herbert made love to a beautiful young woman who, he says, taught him "the great truth of love's consummation, which is that the male's part is not to satisfy his own superficial lust so much, as to rouse the deep desire of which the female is capable, and see to satisfying that as a privilege for being desired."[17] It is this discovery that is at the heart of many of the concerns of *Poor Fellow My Country*.

In addition to his own romantic affairs there was also at this time Herbert's equally revealing response to public events, especially the nationwide strike of 1917, over the question whether Australians should be conscripted to fight for England in World War I. Herbert's political confusion (if one wants to describe it uncharitably), or anarchism (if one is prepared to dignify it with the status of an ideology), is nowhere better exemplified than in the account of his reaction to that event.

Caught up mostly by the excitement, and largely ignorant of the political and moral issues at stake, the young Herbert joined the National Volunteers (or National Scabs, as the strikers called them) who were attempting to break up the strike. As usual, Herbert overcame the sneers and derision of his fellow cadets with the one weapon he was learning to use more and more effectively at this time—his fists. Only after demonstrating his pugilistic prowess could he offer his lofty intellectual rationalization—that he could not, in fact, be scabbing on his fellow workers because he was not a member of the working class. "Not of the working class!," the older Herbert comments ruefully of the younger one. "What a difference had been wrought in me by good clothes, genteel company, and not having that common workingman, my father, around to cramp my style."[18] Only a later experience of humiliation with a treacherous upper class friend named Cyril Bumbert brought home to him the folly of his social pretensions.

But what the incident—as well as a later political crisis—demonstrates is Herbert's essentially apolitical nature as well as his individualistic dislike of collective action. *Poor Fellow My Country* would seem at a superficial glance to be unusual in Herbert's work in that for a considerable time it depicts Jeremy Delacy as attempting to achieve social ends by working through a political party framework (even if it is one he himself erects). But it is clear throughout the novel that this attempt goes against his (and the author's) true instincts and that it is doomed to failure. Jeremy's conception of the nature of political action, like that of his creator, is naive. Neither makes any distinction between Labor and Liberal (i.e., in the misleading Australian political terminology, Conservative) parties, and their political attitudes could be best summed up as the supreme embodiment of the traditional Australian contempt for all politicians, whether of the Right or Left, as "bludgers" and mediocrities.

A similar confusion—Heseltine generously calls it ambivalence—appears in the only other political clash Herbert describes in the volume. In 1919, in the sequel to the events of two years earlier, the former dock workers decided to remove the "scabs" or renegade workers who had taken their jobs from them, and police from Perth were sent to maintain authority and read the Riot Act. The police shot one of the workers down before prudently retiring to the protection of their headquarters. Herbert, whose aversion to his old friends, the National Volunteers, had grown in the past two years, was at first happy to join the roaring mob who forced the Volunteers to flee and dumped the contents of their well-furnished offices in the river.

The next day, however, the dock workers were still restlessly wandering the streets, demanding that the police give up the representative among them who had shot and killed their comrade. Whispers began to be heard of a lynch mob. With somewhat foolhardy courage, Herbert stood up and defended the police to the crowd as only doing their duty. A short time later, however, he found the crowd had trapped four policemen and looked likely to beat them to death. He waded in to help but was in danger of being killed himself when one of the crowd stopped the others with the magic Australian talisman of an expression "Fair go!" only to turn upon Herbert himself and administer an enormous beating.

In the meantime the police had used this diversion to regroup and to summon up reinforcements. The final irony came when a detective, who had called on Herbert and his parents, not only failed to praise him, as Herbert fondly expected, but actually criticized him for being on the streets at all after the Riot Act had been read. The only praise he won was from the docker who had stopped the crowd from beating him in order to do so democratically himself, and whom Herbert met a week later. As so often in *Disturbing Element*, a fight was a way of cementing a bond between the two combatants, this time over a couple of ritualistic pots, Herbert's first beers, in fact. The paradoxical reactions of the policemen he had saved and the docker he had fought with had one other effect: they finally made clear to Herbert where his true allegiance lay. He concludes the episode with the words:

I recall the thrill of discovering that I truly belonged to the working class and of my swearing to vindicate myself for having allowed myself to be led to betrayal of my heritage by that daughter of a hundred alien earls, my mother.[19]

Henceforth, he remained constant in his hatred of that English inspired war he had at one stage almost run away to join, and in his traditionally Australian, convict inspired loathing of the police, a sentiment best summed up in the phrase one of the rioting crowd hurled at him, and which he was later to use as the title for a short story: "Once a policeman, never a man!"

IV   Journey East

In the meantime, Herbert, frightened into virtuous industry by a practical joke played on him by friends who had discovered his romantic exploits, had at last passed his Preliminary Pharmaceutical and had gone to work as an apprentice to a Mr. Charles Huggister, M.P.S. As with most of the bosses he worked for, Herbert was totally unable to get along with Huggister. According to this account of him the man was a lecherous old charlatan, specializing in venereal matters about which he knew next to nothing and for which therefore he could offer clients only spurious hope. Although Herbert did learn something about pharmacy despite his employer, most of his energy at this time appears to have gone into a long succession of sexual exploits. At first, suffering under the delusion that only thus could he prove his manhood, he visited a series of brothels but was unable to avail himself of the services offered until he met the previously mentioned Aboriginal girl, Jilgie, whom he had known as a child. Later his adventurings were with a series of more "respectable" girls, including the daughter of the police sergeant whom he had gone to assist during the riots; with this girl he had a protracted and painful relationship.

At the age of twenty he sat for his final examinations and passed everything except the practical Dispensing Test, for which supplementary section he had to wait six months to sit. He quit the pharmacist, however, but then after a brief friendship with a drunken doctor decided that pharmacy was not enough and that he wanted to study medicine. To the rage of his parents, who had at last begun to see a prosperous career ahead for him, he returned to study in order to pass matriculation. Oddly enough, it had been only shortly before this, in the throes of his unhappy affair with the sergeant's daughter, that he had begun to read and enjoy novels for the first time. After his brother Phil had gone East and sent back word that there were many opportunities available over "T' other side" he decided to follow him. Shortly after arriving in Melbourne, Herbert landed a job as dispenser in the city's biggest hospital.

Not even the long flight east was enough to free Herbert from his family, and especially his mother who was still determined that he should buy a chemist's shop, marry and settle down. He took a flat with Phil, whom he was supporting at the time, but they were quickly joined by his half-sister Bridget and young brother Bill, and then came word that his mother was coming over to see him, and later his father also (after selling up everything he owned in the West). The family worked systematically at inveigling him into accepting the shop while at the same time pretending to understand and sympathize completely with his abandonment of interest in a career of pharmacy.

Herbert went along with the plan for a while, ostensibly until he passed his matriculation, but he was living on borrowed time. In his effort to make money quickly, he was indulging in some dubious practices involving cures and was reported to the Pharmaceutical Council by a jealous competitor. Although he escaped with a fine, he was already losing what little interest he had in the business, until when he sat for and passed matriculation he told his parents flatly that he was no longer prepared to run it. At the same time he was becoming increasingly interested in the possibilities of writing fiction and actually had some work published under the pseudonym, Herbert Astor in a contemporary periodical, *The Australian Journal*. Even as he entered medical school, Herbert was increasingly doubtful as to the likelihood of his completing it. His few months in medical school were actually spent in romantic dalliances of a now familiar kind, in generally horsing around, and at one stage in a rather ingenious exposure of a group of medical charlatans (perhaps in penitence for his own earlier, brief indulgence in quackery). When the examinations came around at the end of the year he took them but with no expectation of, or even desire for, success. As he writes:

I was done with medicine. My true study, I decided, was life, my true vocation the interpretation of my observations through the dramaturgy of the written word, and my school for this was the whole wide world.[20]

Once again, Xavier Herbert had detached himself from his family and surroundings.

V *Wanderings*

So much for the formative years. *Disturbing Element*, that most unusual "Portrait of the Artist as a Young Man," ends there, with Herbert on board ship, waving goodbye to his father and his girl friend, each comically unaware of the other's presence, and feeling free for the first time in his life. The rest of his life is much less well documented and if it is true, as he has claimed, that *Poor Fellow My Country* is the last novel he intends to write, then one hopes at least that the autobiography can be continued and that the rest of it will be as spirited and unsparing of himself as *Disturbing Element* is.

After leaving Melbourne Herbert travelled to Sydney where he stayed for a while. He spent approximately a year in Sydney, then travelled North, on the way discovering the little town of Redlynch, near Cairns, Queensland, where twenty years later he was to settle. He told John Hetherington in an interview, "I thought Redlynch the most beautiful place I ever saw . . . and that if I settled anywhere it would be there."[21] Although Herbert during this time never seems to have lost his ambition of becoming a writer the rest of this decade was spent scarcely at all in writing but rather in wandering all over Australia, gathering experience and trying his hand at a number of occupations. As he puts it rather proudly in his "Autobiographette":

> . . . I have roamed the length and breadth of our island continent. I have thirsted on the dry Barcoo, hungered on the flooded Yarra, seen the sunrise over Karri in the hills of Mundijong and seen it set behind the emu-plains on the track to Willeroo. I have cut sleepers in the mountains of North Queensland, mustered cattle on the Rankine Plains, fossicked for gold on the Barrington Tops, lived with the blacks on the Daly, dived for pearl-shell in the Timor Sea, slept in the Domain in Sydney, picked waratahs at Gosford, boronia at Childow's Well, wattle in the Dandenongs, swum in the Murray River, hunted in the Flinders Range—and the result is that I have become religious, imbued with a measureless spiritual love for the living land that bore me.[22]

It was an unconventional education for an aspiring young writer but on the whole an effective, and in Herbert's case, perhaps even a necessary one. In *Disturbing Element*, Herbert mentions an incident in which a friend who believed he was wasting his time pursuing a medical career urged him to write down the stories he had been recounting. Herbert describes his response:

> He was always trying to get me to write what I so eagerly told him of my experiences. But I could see no point in such writing . . .
>
> He wanted me particularly to write what he called Stories of my early life. I would not, could not. To me a Story was something made up. It still is.[23]

Perhaps so. And yet it does not take very much acquaintance with Herbert's work to see how deeply the stories he tells come from his own very considerable experience; and the adventures of the nineteen twenties—working as drover, stockrider, prison overseer, fettler, pearl diver, railway ganger, living in Queensland and visiting the Solomon and Gilbert Islands as well as Fiji, before finally ending up in Darwin in the Northern Territories—were invaluable in giving him the material on which he drew for *Capricornia* and *Poor Fellow My Country* especially.

In 1930 he finally left Darwin and sailed to England, en route writing his first short novel, *Black Velvet*. (Black Velvet was the name whites gave to sexual dealings with the Aborigines.) Although it was to be his first and last visit overseas (the Pacific Island wanderings excepted) it was also one of the most vitally important periods in his life.

According to Camden Morrisby, Herbert claimed to have started off in the West End of London and finished up in a doss-house in the East End.[24] He was unable to interest any publisher in *Black Velvet*. His account of it to Patricia Rolfe in an interview is as follows:

"They found it too harsh," he said. But I said, "I come from a harsh country." They said, "There's nobody any good in it." I said, "There was nobody any good where I came from and I was no better than the rest."[25]

He supported himself marginally by writing short stories and scenarios. More importantly he met a young milliner named Sadie Norden and fell in love with her. Impressed by the tales he told of the North of Australia and, like others, divining the young man's talent for storytelling she urged him to write it all down.

Thus began *Capricornia*. Herbert gave an account of the writing of the novel in a speech to the Adelaide Arts Festival in 1962, which was subsequently reprinted in *Australian Literary Studies*.[26] Herbert's remarkable working routine involved writing for up to thirty-two hours at a stretch, then sleeping for sixteen. All this time Sadie looked after him with completely selfless devotion, coming into his room to clean it up or bring him meals while he worked away, so obsessed with the book he was writing that he was almost oblivious to her presence. But he had no more commercial success with *Capricornia* than he had had with *Black Velvet*. Publishers were sympathetic but found it too much of a rough diamond (as well as

far too long, no doubt), although Herbert has claimed that he could
have had it published in England

> ... then and there by Jonathan Cape (Gilchrist Thompson was the
> managing publisher at the time) had I agreed to the cutting out of what
> was considered to be offensively Australian in it and could I have stood any
> more of that awful climate.[27]

Instead, Herbert returned to Australia (by bicycle and tramp
steamer) and has since kept his vow never to travel overseas again.
Over the next twelve months, in a frantic effort to both support
himself and bring Sadie out from England he wrote for *Smith's
Weekly* and churned out formula short stories for *The Australian
Journal* and *The Sydney Sun* at an astonishingly productive rate,
twenty-two stories in 1933 alone, according to his letters. The best
of these were later gathered together and published as a collection
under the title *Larger Than Life*. Then, when Sadie finally joined
him, according to Morrisby he "dug himself in at Narrabeen and
rewrote the entire book twice. Six months it took him."[28] In the
same year he met P. R. Stephensen, who had just returned from
England also, and who accepted the manuscript of *Capricornia*
instantly.

VI   *Stephensen and the Publication of* Capricornia

Perry Reginald ("Inky") Stephensen was a man of some intellectual distinction, a Rhodes Scholar from Queensland and author of
the book, *The Foundations of Culture in Australia* (1936). He was
also a racist of a most offensive kind.[29] Born in 1901 (the same year
as Herbert) Stephensen in his undergraduate days was a radical and
early member of the Communist Party. After studying at Oxford
University, Stephensen stayed on in England and became associated
with a number of small presses such as Fanfrolico and Mandrake,
which published small, expensive, high quality editions of significant literary works, including *Lady Chatterley's Lover*, Lawrence's
paintings, and works by such Australian writers as Norman and Jack
Lindsay, Hugh McCrae and Kenneth Slessor. His magazine *London
Aphrodite* published Aldous Huxley, Rhys Davies, Liam O'Flaherty,
T. F. Powers and the Australian writer Brian Penton during its brief
existence. Stephensen's own meagre verse and fiction are mediocre
and it was in his roles as publisher, critic and patron of other writers
that he appears to have made most impact. In 1932 he returned to
Australia a few months ahead of Herbert. He spent one year with

the Endeavour Press, which was financed by *The Bulletin* magazine, but left when his initial contract expired to set up his own publishing firm, P. R. Stephensen and Co. By this time he had become a somewhat rabid patriot and nationalist.

The extent to which Stephensen was responsible firstly for the actual fact of *Capricornia* being published and secondly for the form which it finally took is a controversial question and the exact truth is difficult to ascertain. In March, 1961, a fierce debate broke out in the pages of *The Bulletin*, sparked off by Herbert's indignation at a remark by another Australian writer Olaf Ruhen that Stephensen's assistance to Xavier Herbert in the production of *Capricornia* was meticulous and detailed, and extended over a matter of months. The argument ended indecisively, with Herbert angrily promising to produce proof that "NO ONE EDITED *Capricornia* BUT MY-SELF."[30] A few months later Herbert gave the speech to the Adelaide Festival of Arts quoted from earlier and concluded by saying, "So much then for the writing of old *Capricornia*. The story of its publication is quite another and a stranger one by far. Perhaps I may get back here to tell it."[31]

Unfortunately, he never did, but as far as one can sort it out the story is as follows. The original typescript of the novel, completed in England, ran to something on the order of one million words. Herbert claims that it was shown to only one English publisher in that form. Stephensen, on the other hand, who claims it was rejected by eleven English publishers gives no evidence for that unlikely story. Possibly he was confusing the novel with the earlier *Black Velvet*. In an elaboration of his remarks to Patricia Rolfe quoted earlier Herbert states:

I took the massive typescript to Jonathan Cape, where there was a man I knew, one Gilchrist Thompson, who had shown more interest in "Black Velvet" than anyone else and predicted that someday I would do something good. Gilchrist Thompson declared that I had done the something good in that *Capricornia*, but had done it too lavishly. Apart from the fact that it was commercially impossible to publish such a large book, he gave it as his opinion that it was otherwise spoilt by its prolixity. He advised me to set it aside for a year, and in that year to write short stories for magazines as exercise in conciseness, then to write the book again. Thompson offered to help me make contact with magazine editors there in England, and personally to see that I shouldn't want.[32]

At any rate, although grateful for Thompson's advice, Herbert feeling he could not bear England any longer, returned to Australia.

There he took the manuscript of the novel to Stephensen and the Endeavour Press, which expressed interest but claimed it would need rewriting and considerable compression. Herbert eventually recovered the manuscript from Norman Lindsay, one of Stephensen's codirectors in the company. Herbert himself claims, in one of the more outrageous venturings of the self-styled "Romantic liar," that he reclaimed it from a rubbish dump! Stephensen says that Herbert then presented it to the leading Australian publishing company, Angus & Robertson, who rejected it as too lengthy. The author has not denied this story, which is certainly consistent with the publishing record of Angus & Robertson at the time.

Then Herbert apparently again took the novel to Stephensen, now with his own company in Bond Street, Sydney. Because it was so long Stephensen unwisely agreed to let Herbert tell him the story of the novel from beginning to end instead of reading it for himself, and so began one of those now legendary Herbert marathon monologues. Acting partly under Stephensen's suggestions, Herbert rewrote and cut the book, Stephensen began to set it in type, but when it was three quarters set the company went into voluntary liquidation. Stephensen alleges that he then showed the completed galleys to Walter Cousins of Angus & Robertson who (again?) rejected it as "too lengthy." The two tons of type were melted down and Herbert in the intensity of his disappointment "went bush"— leaving his home for the solitude of the inland and finishing up eventually in Darwin, where he took on a succession of jobs, including working a tantalie mining lease on the Darwin River, and becoming superintendent of the Darwin Aboriginal Compound, which he mentions frequently in his letters of the time. Unfortunately, despite the efforts of a Professor Elkin to get him the job on a permanent basis, Herbert was eased out of it by the authorities on grounds that he lacked the academic qualification of a Diploma of Anthropology.

In the meantime, Stephensen had become associated with W. J. Miles in the formation of The Publicist Publishing Company, with a shop in the T. and G. Building, Sydney. He resumed the effort to publish *Capricornia* and this time was successful. Although "1938" appears on the title page of the novel, Stephensen actually folded, sewed and bound one copy by hand, and lodged it with the organisers of a competition for "the best novel published, or accepted for publication in Australia in 1937" twenty-four hours before entries were due to close on December 31st. Three months later the novel was announced as the winner of the Sesquicentennial Commonwealth Prize worth two hundred and fifty pounds. Later it won the Australian Literature Society's gold medal and in 1940 Herbert was awarded a Commonwealth Literary Fund fellowship. Although sales were slow at first, eventually the novel began to win the kind of critical attention it deserved. Angus & Robertson, generously offered the contract and the standing type at cost price by Stephensen, at last accepted. And so there began the first of many subsequent reprintings. The novel has also been translated into several foreign languages.

So much for the saga of how *Capricornia* came to be published. Two conclusions from this involved history can, perhaps, be drawn with some confidence. The first is that Stephensen's persistence and courage in seeing the book through to print, and his generosity in promoting it incessantly in his magazine *The Publicist* in the most glowing terms[33] deserve the highest praise. And indeed Herbert, with not uncharacteristic generosity, has acknowledged this. Even while angrily rejecting Stephensen's claim to having edited the novel he said of him:

> The tremendous thing he did was to show my talent to me myself and to teach me to bend the knee to no one in respect of it. For that I am eternally grateful. Nor should I alone be grateful to "Inky" Stephensen, but every Australian writer with pride in his work, because it was in him our pride originated. Australian writers were just sneaks till "Inky" stood up and yelled for them.[34]

But equally important is that although Stephensen did undoubtedly help to "edit" *Capricornia*, Herbert's claim that Stephensen never wrote a word of the novel is undoubtedly true and is borne out by the manuscript at the National Library, Canberra. The difference is in part a purely semantic one: Herbert clearly ascribes far more weight to the function of editing in the process of creating fiction than more sophisticated writers do, and this is probably the mistaken basis of much of the argument. It seems obvious that Stephensen made suggestions and criticisms of the kind that any editor genuinely interested in the book he is working on would do, and which most writers would take for granted, using them where he felt they were helpful, rejecting them when he thought they were not. The two men's arguments finally peter out in a rather childish quarrel about when and how Herbert acquired Fowler's *Modern English Usage*.

The significance of the argument in terms of Herbert's later career, however, is quite real. There seems no doubt that the circumstances of the novel's publication had a considerable effect on the author and had a great deal to do with his insistence that *Poor Fellow My Country* be published exactly as it was written, at almost the original length of the first version of *Capricornia*.

VII   *Herbert's Later Life*

In personal terms, Herbert's life after 1940 and the success of *Capricornia* has not been as spectacular or turbulent as it was before. For some years he fought in World War II, rising to the rank of sergeant. After the war he returned to Redlynch, the little town near Cairns that he had discovered twenty years before and fallen in love with, and he and Sadie have lived there ever since. Not only has Herbert kept his word never to go overseas again but he rarely visits even the Australian cities, which he detests. When he does make his brief, periodic "raids" on them, it is usually for a specific purpose—to promote a forthcoming novel, for instance, or to accept some new academic or literary distinction.

Nor has his literary career followed any conventional pattern. Although he wrote prolifically after the publication of *Capricornia* nothing appeared in print, with the exception of a few short magazine pieces, for over twenty years. During that period there were continual promises of new projects under way. I mentioned earlier the entire long novel *Yeller Feller* which he burned because he said it was too like *Capricornia*. There have been other projects— a novel called *The King and the Kurrawaddi* and another called *Sacred to the Memory of the Scrub Bull*—of which the author commented ruefully, "The very titles will show how hopeless was the task for me, a bushie born, doomed to die a bushie."[35] Even the novel that eventually became *Soldiers' Women* passed through a stage when it was known portentously as *Of Mars, the Moon, and Destiny* before fortunately reverting to its original title. Herbert's letters in the National Library are full of enthusiastically described new projects—a novel called *Hai Sei* dealing with the Japanese in Australia, another called *True Commonwealth*, another shorter novel called *Rex versus Dingo Jo*. When Herbert took up flying aircraft in the nineteen fifties there were foreshadowings of a novel called *Winged Victory*, while one chapter of an autobiographical novel called *I, the Little Widow, and the World* has been mentioned here also.

During all this time, Herbert lived off the royalties from *Capricornia*, eked out by occasional Commonwealth Literary Fund Grants (three thousand pounds in 1952, one thousand pounds in 1957). When short of money he would take up one of the various casual occupations at which he is proficient—bacteriologist, union organizer, stockrider, sailor, miner, railwayman as well as flyer—and he continues to employ occasionally his pharmaceutical skills.

Then in 1959 came the spectacular renaissance, with four more books, beginning with *Seven Emus,* appearing within the space of five years. As with most of Herbert's books, the publication of *Seven Emus* was surrounded by controversy. According to Herbert in his article "I Sinned Against Syntax" he had by this time written *Soldiers' Women* using a highly eccentric system of punctuation of his own devising. He explains it thus:

Actually my sentences were not unduly long, and were more markedly divided than by the conventional method, because *two* steps were used instead of one. My own precious syntactical system demanded that a paragraph consist of an entity of the whole composition that was self-contained and hence could have but one initial capital and one concluding stop. Pauses between parts of this entity, which conventionally would be marked with a full stop, were marked with two points, thus .. I believed that by my system emotion could be better expressed than with the conventional, which would demand conventional reading.[36]

But publishers were allegedly prepared to accept the novel only if Herbert restored conventional punctuation. According to Herbert, Beatrice Davis, executive editor of Angus & Robertson and one of the most distinguished editors Australia has produced, then:

... somehow divined that I would never be convinced of the unacceptability of the affectation that I was calling originality until I had been tried and condemned for it through publication. To this end she encouraged me to write *Seven Emus* "in the style"—meaning the style of the Botch— assuring me that what I wrote would be faithfully printed to the comma. I could never have put pen to paper again to write creatively except on those terms.[37]

The novel was greeted with almost unanimous critical disapproval or at best lack of enthusiasm, which the author tended to blame on the outraged sensibilities of critics at his sins against syntax. As I try to show in Chapter five, however, the failings of the book are far more radical than this account suggests and the whole issue of punctuation strikes me as rather a red herring. I agree completely with Heseltine's view that "the prose of *Seven Emus* does not transmit a significantly more intense emotion than if it had been conventionally punctuated."[38] The upshot of it was that Herbert went back to his wartime novel, rewrote it and restored its original, simpler title as well as conventional punctuation. He says:

> I was able to tear the Botch of Botches to bits and sit down to rewrite it as a story pure and simple. What took me three-and-a-half years to write in solitude I rewrote back in the noisy lovely world in three-and-a-half months. Significantly it became *Soldiers' Women* again.[39]

Again its reviews were not noticeably complimentary.

Herbert professes to having never been worried about either his long silence after *Capricornia* or the mixed critical reputation his subsequent work has received. He points constantly to the greater pleasures he derives from such feats as the winning of his flying spurs, or to the harmony of his relationship with his wife, of whom he speaks invariably in admiring and generous terms, and to his friendships with the "ordinary," unintellectual people of Redlynch. As *Seven Emus* demonstrates, he has a deep ambivalence towards, if not active dislike of, most academics and excepts from this dislike only those academics who have assisted him in his work such as Hergenhan and Heseltine.

There is in this, though, a certain disingenuous element. Herbert has shown extreme sensitivity to the view of him (essentially the one offered here) as a one-book writer. He dislikes intensely those critical views of him which see his greatness as resting primarily on *Capricornia*, with subsequent work being inferior to this; indeed he is himself inclined to speak patronizingly or dismissively of that novel.

Moreover, for all his apparent indifference towards success, he is not above promoting the publication of his major novels in a shrewd and hardheaded way. (Nor, I hasten to add, is there any reason why he should be.) Each of his three long novels was launched with a good deal of fanfare and publicity and there is no doubt that this has assisted in the strong (and continuing) sales of all three.

For the publication of *Soldiers' Women* and *Poor Fellow My Country* he emerged from his Queensland isolation, travelled to the big cities he hates, and delivered himself loudly and publically of the views he has formed over the years. For *Poor Fellow My Country* he presented a very high profile indeed, writing articles in the newspapers and giving many interviews, appearing on television and, after receiving the Miles Franklin award for the best Australian novel of the year, delivering an aggressive and iconoclastic speech of acceptance to the audience at the Victorian Fellowship of Australian Writers annual dinner.

The extent to which, unlike his hero Jeremy Delacy, he is prepared to compromise can be seen from the circumstances of the publication of that novel. As Herbert himself rather uneasily explains,[40] his fifty-year war against "imperial publishers" came to an end with the signing of a contract with William Collins, the English publishers and "absentee landlords" of precisely the type at which he himself rails in the novel.

CHAPTER 2

Capricornia

TO summarize the plot of *Capricornia*, a huge, apparently sprawling novel about an area of Northern Australia, is next to impossible. Although in fact the novel is neatly structured as well as carefully defined in terms of both time and space, so much happens in the way of violent deaths, railway smashes, floods and long treks that at first there seems little order to it at all. However, *Capricornia* has two central and related stories that occupy most of the foreground of its attention.

The first of these is the story of the Shillingsworth family and especially of Norman, son of Mark Shillingsworth by a black girl; it includes not only Norman, however, but also his father and his uncle and foster father Oscar, and Mark's lover Heather Shay. Although the various Shillingsworths tend to disappear from the novel at various times, they always come back into it again. The novel takes their history from 1904, when they first arrive in Capricornia, to somewhere near the actual date of the novel's publication in 1937, by which time Oscar is dead and Mark, Heather and Norman are finally united and planning tentatively to leave the country.

There are large gaps in this history, times when one or other of the characters goes down South and virtually disappears from the novel or, like Mark, is forced to "go bush" and adopt a new identity. Mark, for instance, disappears after his murder of Cho Kee See at the end of chapter nine and does not reappear until some one hundred and seventy-five pages later as Jack Ramble, whose real identity the reader guesses long before his son does. Oscar similarly goes South towards the end of World War I (Herbert is extremely cynical about his motives) and does not return into the novel until chapter seventeen, some sixty-five pages later, by which time he is fifty-four years old and it is 1928. We learn virtually nothing about what either he or Norman did "down South." As the title suggests, this is a novel about a single, peculiar and well-defined region and once a character disappears from it the author tends largely to lose interest in him.

While the Shillingsworth characters recede from the foreground the novel concentrates on a second main theme and group of characters who have an obvious bearing on the main ones. The initial connecting figure is Oscar, with his decision to reject the dying Peter Differ's plea to save his half-caste daughter Connie; the concluding connection is with Norman and his relationship with Tocky.

As often in the novel, Herbert makes his judgments not explicitly but though structure and placement. The whole subordinate motif of Connie through to Tocky and her dead baby is one of several comparisons the author makes (Ket, on whom a great deal of focus is placed in the latter stages of the novel, is another) between Norman and other characters who, though in a similar predicament, receive less fortunate treatment. In Norman's case his uncle— initially almost against his will, it is true, but eventually with love— accepts him. Differ's plea, by contrast, he rejects, and as a consequence sets in motion the long series of circumstances that lead to the novel's final, tragic image: that of Tocky and her baby, both dead, having been marooned in an empty water tank from which she was unable to escape. Connie is placed under the protection of the missionary Humbolt Lace, who seduces her, then when he finds out that she is pregnant, attempts to marry her off, first to Yeller Elbert, until he is thrown in jail for the murder of Jock Driver, and then another half-caste by the name of Peter Pan, finally does marry her in exchange for Lace's bribes.

We next meet Connie, dying of consumption and gonorrhea and with a young baby who comes eventually to be known as Tocky, when she is discovered by Tim O'Cannon, one of only three men in the huge list of characters in the novel (the others are Differ and Andy McRandy) who treat the blacks with real understanding and humanity and respect their dignity as human beings. O'Cannon attempts to do with the daughter what Differ attempted with the mother—bring her up so that she has all the benefits and accomplishments of a white education and can marry respectably. The link with the main story is resumed when Norman meets up with Tocky, who has escaped from a missionary camp, during his treks in the wilderness after Oscar's death, and they become lovers. However, Norman, partly because he is never quite able to accept his own Aboriginal heritage, as Prindy does unquestioningly in *Poor Fellow My Country*, can never fully accept Tocky, and this is one of the elements that contribute finally to her death.

I   *Australian Racism*

Capricornia seems at first to be one of those epic saga novels— Brian Penton's *Landtakers* is an example roughly contemporaneous with Herbert's novel, Colleen MacDonough's *The Thorn Birds* the most recent one—so common amongst Australian fiction which document the life of a family over several generations. It does not take long, however, to realize how much more than, and how different from, those and similar novels this is. I mentioned earlier Professor Vincent Buckley's article on the novel and the influence it had on more recent criticism laying stress on the nonrealistic elements in the book. Buckley was no doubt reacting against the earlier, simplistic views of it as essentially an example of social realism.[1]

However, as I also suggested, it is possible that the reaction against this limited social realist interpretation of the novel has swung so far that we are in danger of forgetting simply how much of it is passionately concerned with very specific social abuses and injustices, all of them involving the exploitation of blacks by whites, and with the ambiguous half-castes such as Norman, Tocky, Charles Ket, and Yeller Elbert and their varying reactions to the refusal of the whites to give them a decent position in society.

The whole of the first chapter, even to its vituperative title "The Coming of the Dingoes," makes the general point of which innumerable examples will later be given. The tone is one of apparently objective, historical narration, laced with heavy irony at the expense of the forces of so-called "civilization," a word that recurs again and again in the novel with increasingly resonant irony. The chapter is imbued with a sense of violence. Herbert speaks impassively of the appropriately named Treachery Bay (afterwards, he points out, changed to New Westminster) being set up on "what was perhaps the most fertile and pleasant part of the coast and on the bones of half the Karrapillua Tribe," and a moment later repeats the suggestion: "The site of Port Zodiac was a Corroboree Ground of the Larrapuna Tribe, who left the bones of most of their number to manure it."[2] He refers to the violence of the climate as well, significantly says of a particular island that it "lay within rifle-shot of the mainland" and, in speaking of the coming of the white man, the event with which the book opens, says, "Nature is cruel. When dingoes come to a water-hole, the ancient kangaroos, not having teeth or ferocity sharp enough to defend their heritage, must relinquish it or die."[3] The analogy is not difficult to grasp, and in any case Herbert spells it out not long afterwards: chapter four, which tells of the demise of Ned Krater, is headed "Death of a Dingo."

The novel's subject matter, then, is very much the racism that is so much a part of Australia's history and arguably an intrinsic part of the Australian's character; and specifically the whites' appalling mistreatment of the blacks. Herbert has made clear, both in his later fiction and in certain polemical writings, his lifelong and passionate concern with this issue. Nevertheless, Buckley's intuition is essentially correct that the novel is very much more than a polemic. Throughout the novel Herbert is very careful to define the world of Capricornia, both in terms of time and space—a world he eventually establishes as both fact and metaphor—and metaphor precisely because, as in *Moby Dick*, Capricornia in fact is so carefully and meticulously "documented" fact.

The first sentence of the novel includes the phrase "that northern part of the Continent of Australia which is called Capricornia," thus defining the area of the world with which the novel will be concerned very clearly; and throughout the novel Herbert employs fictitious but clearly identifiable names for the various areas of Australia he discusses—Port Zodiac for Darwin, for instance, Cooksland (Queensland), Batman (Melbourne), Churchtown (Adelaide) and so on. Those critics who are puzzled because he does not use the actual names while nevertheless making them so easily identifiable miss the point completely: Though careful to define the area of about half a million square miles that he is dealing with, Herbert does not want to suggest that he is merely chronicling the history of the North of Australia. The fictive territory of Capricornia is both physical and metaphysical. It comes to be the vehicle for what is essentially a moral and metaphysical vision: of man (or at least white man) as aggressive, anomalous being, alienated from a nature which is above all bountiful and, although sometimes violent and apparently treacherous, also ethically neutral, dispassionate, dangerous mostly to those who do not accept its objective existence but attempt to subvert it or conquer it.

II   *Nature in Capricornia*

There is a moment in *Capricornia* when Tim O'Cannon is journeying down the railway on a trike. The tone of Herbert's description, while comic, is also redolent of the richness and bounty of nature, its abundant vitality:

He trundled on, up grade and down, through dripping cuttings where golden catch-fly orchids grew in mossy nooks and tadpoles wriggled in sparkling pools, over culverts where smooth brown water sped over beds of grass, past towering walls of weeds that stretched out leaves and flowers to tickle his face and shower him with dew and touch him—as though he were a flower to be fertilised!—with blobs of pollen. He trundled on, up grade and down, keeping one eye on the permanent way, the other on the telegraph—the Transcontinental Telegraph, strand of copper linking Australia with the world, shimmering plaything of the sun and wind, live-thing humming as if to occupy itself in loneliness with repeating gossip of the lives it linked—keeping one eye on that and the other on the per-way, looking for defects, but not so sedulously as to miss any passing fancy.

A kangaroo leapt off the road and thud-thud-thudded into silence. A family of kangaroos, same number as the O'Cannons and about the same size, bounded ahead through a cutting. A buffalo dozing in Chinaman's Creek woke with a start and bolted. A shower of white cockatoos fell out of a bloodwood tree, yelling, "A man—a man—a Disturbing Element!" A large admiral lizard leapt up on a rail, stood on hind legs with fore legs raised like hands and watched for a moment that trundling Thing, then loped down the cess-path with arms swinging and iridescent frill flying out like a cape, looking for all the world like a bandy old admiral of days of Drake.[4]

Disturbing Element we have seen is the title of Herbert's autobiography and this passage helps to define what the term means for him. In the world of *Capricornia* man is indeed the primary disturbing element. While aloof and impersonal, impervious to ethical considerations, nature for Herbert is also flourishing and bountiful and it is only man who is an anomoly, at war with his kind and environment. Herbert goes out of his way again and again in the novel to stress the ethical neutrality of nature. When Ned Krater dies, the ants get to his body before the awed natives can summon up enough courage to approach it. "The crocodiles, being respecters neither of persons nor of devils, came and rooted him out and devoured him as soon as they discovered where he lay."[5] At the funeral of Jock Driver, "When the coffin was lifted from the hearse three blow-flies shot out of the holes in the lid and dashed off guiltily."[6] When Norman was alone with nature for the first time "He sought companionship of stars that formerly had been as familiar as street lamps, to find them strange, utterly strange, vastly remote, infinite, arranged now to form mysterious designs of frightening significance."[7] The tone of authorial detachment and omniscience that characterizes the novel as a whole is never so insistently and consciously present as when Herbert is describing what he calls "nature's contrariety to man"[8] and man's ignorance of the workings of nature. Throughout Norman's trek through the Wet in chapter twenty-two, for instance, Herbert dwells continually with a kind of grim relish on the mistakes that Norman makes, and the danger in which he places himself by his ignorance of the violent but perfectly explicable weather. Exactly the same tone is adopted but to an even greater extent during the account of Ket's panic stricken flight from the law.

Nature, then, can be impersonally dangerous and destructive; but more often the emphasis of the novel is placed on its neverending richness and vitality. As the Aboriginal Bootpolish puts it to Norman after his frightening and near fatal journey, "Proper good country dis one. Plenty kangaroo, plenty buffalo, plenty bandicoot, plenty yam, plenty goose, plenty duck, plenty lubra, plenty corroboree, plenty fun, plenty ebrythings. Number-one good country."[9] It is "Arcady" in chapter twenty-eight, where paradisical overtones are constantly present. The Aborigines called the site of Port Zodiac "Mailunga, or the Birth Place, believing it to be a sort of Garden of Eden and apparently revering it."[10]

Again, throughout the trek of little Tocky O'Cannon, yet another of the many journeys in which the novel abounds, Herbert makes much of the natural richness of the country and the ease with which she is able to live off frogs' legs, gooseberries, honey and crystal water—although, on the other hand, there are also marsh-flies, mosquitoes and leeches which drain humans' blood. This even-handed justice is epitomized in the anecdote of the Anopheles mosquito. For once Capricornia is blessed with perfect weather conditions which produce great prosperity—as well as the malaria carrying mosquito, usually kept away by the brutality of the climate.

Similarly, when Mark Shillingsworth builds an electric generator Herbert remarks that "Unfortunately, owing to the perversity of Nature, the tide was usually not running when the light was most required."[11] But an important distinction has to be made here.

Although the author speaks of its "perversity" here, nature is in fact
perfectly consistent, if not predictable; it is Mark who has failed to
adapt to it, utilize it and exploit its laws in such a way as to remain
in harmony with it. The same is true of the punkah "which worked
automatically when the wind blew, that is when its working was not
required."[12] These are instances of human folly at work, or at least
human inability to adjust to nature; but as Norman demonstrates
with his device for catching water from the sweating rocks, this is by
no means an innately necessary thing. Herbert expresses his sense of
the ethical neutrality of nature at one point in generalized form:
"Prosperity is like the tide, being able to flood one shore only by
ebbing from another."[13] It is man who is unable to adjust to this,
and who is anomalous—or more specifically, it needs to be said
again, white man, since Herbert shows the Aboriginals living in
perfect harmony with their environment prior to "The Coming of
the Dingoes" in 1885.

III   The Isolation of Capricornia

The abundance of the natural world of Capricornia is one
important element; another is its isolation, and distance from other
communities, symbolized in the passage quoted above with "the
telegraph—the Transcontinental Telegraph, strand of copper linking Australia with the world, shimmering plaything of the sun and
wind, live-thing humming as if to occupy itself in loneliness with
repeating gossip of the lives it linked," and more pervasively
through the novel by means of the railway. The huge area of
Capricornia is governed by laws of its own which make it unique,
and mark it out from the areas down South, with their carefully
identifiable names.

It is perhaps a corollary of the extreme isolation of the world of
Capricornia from other communities that its inhabitants feel themselves to be a special race of people, with a strong allegiance,
however ambivalent at times, to the particular community in which
they live. That community's sense of its own identity and its
geographical isolation are inextricably linked: "To reach civilization
and the chance to enjoy their spoils," Herbert reminds us of the
fleeing Frank and Ket, "they must travel in a straight line for at
least a thousand miles. To reach civilization unmolested they must
travel many thousand miles."[14] At the same time, though, there is a
constant awareness of that vast remote world to the South of
Capricornia and the latter's dependence on it. One of the reasons

for Herbert's meticulous documentation of dates is no doubt to remind us that, however much Capricornians feel themselves to be members of a separate world, that world is subject to the fortunes and vicissitudes of other worlds many thousands of miles away, by a combination of elements within and without their control. In particular, the two events that affect the lives of Capricornians in the course of the novel are the specific one of the outbreak of war, and the continuing one of varying seasonal conditions: both of these affect the unstable demand for their exports, especially meat.

In chapter eight, entitled "Venus and Mars in Ascendancy," Herbert dates the time of the novel at 1914 with his brief remark that "According to reports from South, Australian beef was being exported as fast as butchered at prices high and in quantities large as never before. Butchery was the order of the day just then. A great war had broken out in Europe."[15] He is openly contemptuous of the Capricornians for allowing themselves to become embroiled in it: "Thus, Capricornia, freest and happiest land on earth, was dragged into a war between kings and queens and plutocrats and slaves and homicidal half-wits, which was being waged in a land in another Hemisphere, thirteen thousand miles away."[16] It is worth noting incidentally that here, as elsewhere in the novel, Herbert reserves his crudest and most moralistic irony for generalities rather than for describing any particular one of his characters, one of the many differences between this novel and *Poor Fellow My Country*. Even at that, however, he is not averse to casting aspersions on the motives of particular individuals as well, as when he tartly remarks of Oscar that he decided to join the war "to be one of the number going to Keep the Home Fires Burning in a good soft job."[17] So eager, in fact, are men to join in the violence that Chook Henn can quote the *Catch-22*-like case of one volunteer:

You know Sam Stiff? Well, he's got miner's complaint he got down in the West so bad he can hardly talk. Course they wouldn't look at him here. So he went down South and got away right off and got killed. Shows what you can do if you can only get down South.[18]

These are cases of human folly, but as usual in the case of Capricornians such folly is compounded by elements over which they genuinely have little or no control, such as climatic conditions there and elsewhere, and notably in "Argostinia" (presumably Argentina):

Good times came to Capricornia when bad times went to the Argostinian Republic. The bovine beasts of Argostinia, which country had been given the trade with the Philipines that was lost to Capricornia through the misdeeds of the *S.S. Cucuracha*, were stricken with foot-and-mouth disease. Then an ill-wind blew upon the Australian States of Cooksland and Sturt, blasting their cattle with the pleura. Thus it became the business of Capricornia to supply beef not only to the Philippines, and not only to the Southern States, but, since all the great beef-exporting countries were now out of business, to a large part of the beef-eating world. Capricornians were staggered. "Where's the catch?" they gasped.[19]

There is no catch, but the important element to understand is the randomness and lack of purpose behind their new prosperity. It is not produced by efforts of their own but simply by chance and can disappear as arbitrarily as it arrived—as indeed, it eventually does. But if financially the Capricornians can be affected by the outside world, *emotionally* it is very rare for them to actually experience this connection; it penetrates no deeper core of their being.

Towards the end of the novel Herbert notes that "Most men had come to think that it would be a shame to open that happy land to fizzling tourists and touts for real estate"[20] and this strong sense of kinship to the land is felt by most of the characters. Norman, for instance, comes to Capricornia intending to stay only a short time. But once he arrives his sense of kinship with the place is immediately felt, despite the ill-treatment he often receives (and he ignores the pleas of his uncle and half-sister Marigold to return to Batman). Even the characters who want to leave Capricornia for the most part fail to do so. The novel is punctuated by a series of attempted escapes which are unsuccessful, and wanderings which are aimless— Mark and Chook, Norman, Tocky, Ket, Frank McLash. The rare exceptions are Humbolt Lace, who escapes to the South, never to be heard of again in the novel, and Oscar's wife Jasmine, who elopes to the Philippines with the captain of the cattle-steamer *Cucuracha*, to disappear eventually into the United States. But the *Cucuracha* itself eventually goes down, as does Mark and Chook's boat, *The Spirit of the Land*. The culmination of all these futile journeys is reached in chapter twenty-eight, which consists of a maze of misunderstandings, mistakes and accidental encounters, with each of the characters misinterpreting the intentions of the others as they blunder into each others' paths, and Herbert standing aloof, outside the consciousness of all of them, and pointing to their mistakes in almost gleefully ironic tones.

The logical solution to the isolation and self-enclosedness of the world of the novel, at least for those not pursued by the law, would seem to lie in the extension of the railway system. But trains, which are another continually recurring motif of the novel, are always associated with destruction. To the Aboriginals, the train is a devil, "a Dibil-dibil" and our first glimpse of the train is through the terrified consciousness of young Norman to whom it is a living monster:

He crawled out warily. Nothing in sight to right or left. When he looked at Anna again his heart ached with love for her. He slowly rose, and rising glanced to right to see—Horror!—the Thing rushing down on him—black hair trailing and white whiskers billowing about its pounding flanks.

He tripped over a rail. The Thing yelled at him. He echoed it with all his might, shot to his feet, raced to the embankment, pitched headlong down, fell in a heap, shot up again, crashed through the scrub, tearing his flesh and scuttling crabs and birds, rushed into the humpy, and shrieking, flung himself into the outstretched arms of Anna.[21]

It is a foretaste of things to come, as is Herbert's introduction of Frank McLash in the following chapter, "The Copper Creek Train," in the remark that "Two years before it had been his ambition to become a first-class criminal; now it was to become the engineer of the Copper Creek train."[22] The ironic point made clearly enough by the impassivity of the tone is spelled out more explicitly not long afterwards: "Frank was one of those creatures that have become so common since his day, a speed-maniac. The Capricornian Railway had great need of such as he."[23]

The series of spectacular mishaps with which the trains are involved reached its culmination in the attempt to extend the railway South and the consequent fatal disaster and abandonment of the project. By 1910, quite early in the novel, the railway system covered one hundred and fifty-seven miles. Approximately twenty years later, when it was finally abandoned, it had advanced only sixty-six miles further. The failure of the scheme is suggestive, too, of the general inability of the Capricornians to control their own lives. It is the white man who is a misfit in this "freest and happiest land on earth" as Herbert describes it, apparently without irony; and he points repeatedly, with either rage or glee or both, to the moral weaknesses that are the reasons for it, the hypocrisy and racism and sheer short-sightedness of their self-interest. "What a world it was in the hands of men!"²⁴ thinks Oscar in a rare moment of introspection, and later, in one of his most brutally explicit outbursts of condemnation, Herbert exclaims, "What a nation! If it ever got anywhere in the world there was no God!"²⁵ Throughout the novel this kind of anguished despair always threatens to break through the fundamental exuberance of the book. By the time of *Poor Fellow My Country* it has won through to become the dominant tone.

IV *Herbert's View of Moral Responsibility*

The example of the railway accidents—especially the last, which is caused by Frank McLash's carelessness—raises the question again that is central to this novel and to Herbert's vision, that of human causality. As Laurie Hergenhan points out in his *Introduction* to the paperback edition of the novel, Herbert takes great pains to emphasize man's culpability in the disasters that befall him. Hergenhan writes:

> It seems to me that Capricornians are basically victims of their own making, including the moulding of social, racial and familial inheritance; injustice is done by men to themselves and others; the Universe and nature go on their way unheeded and unheeding, throwing "the crazy world of man" into relief.²⁶

He goes on to add that "Many 'accidents' (including the railway ones) prove on closer scrutiny to be the results of human negligence and blindness with which life is lived."²⁷

There is a good deal of truth in this and one could even go further in one respect and say that it is not merely the blundering or negligence of the characters but their failures of courage, their hypocrisy and racism and even their brutal aggressiveness that are at the root of their troubles. And yet, it seems to me to fall short of a full understanding of Herbert's vision. If this case is correct what, for instance, is one to make of the scene of the death of Tim O'Cannon?:

> No answer. No answer from any siding. Evidently the Christmas festivities were being generally enjoyed by the train as well as by the sidings. He went back to the tricycle. But before he set out he looked into the houses of his men to wish them the Compliments. None was capable of accepting.

He set out down the gleaming grassy track, today not a rusty one but silver, two slender bars of silver laid on a green velvet mat. He trundled on, bearing his precious burden homeward, feeling not the weight of it on labouring arms and legs, since it was a load of love. He trundled on, caring nothing for the per-way or the T.T.L. today because he was off duty, and nothing for the humming-birds or ants or kangaroos, seeing nothing, hearing nothing, because his thoughts were away at the 58 with his loved ones. He trundled on through dripping cuttings, over roaring culverts, past brooding jungles, under silver hills, he trundled on and on.

From the summit of the 62-Mile bank he caught first glimpse of the white roofs of his homestead, gleaming brightly, a cluster of sails on an ocean of trees. He pulled with renewed vigour, smiling to himself, thinking of those great girls Margaret and Kitty O'Cannon, of those big-kneed youngsters, Bridie and Tocky O'Cannon, of that great ungainly Bloody Parakeet, who would all be there beside the road awaiting him, a hundred times more eagerly than ever, because today he was not merely old Ganger O'Cannon whom they loved for nothing but himself, but old Father Christmas with his swag up. Tocky, he knew, that cheeky kid, would be lying on the cess with ear to rail, listening for the rumble of the trike, which she declared she could hear in that way a distance of two hundred chains, and the rumble of a train at five hundred. Now if fettlers could listen-in to those erratic trains like that—

The smile vanished. His hair leaped under his hat. He turned—and Horror!—saw behind him dashing round a curve an engine. He yelled. He tried to hump from the trike. His foot caught in the load of love. He sprawled back helpless on the carrier. The engine was upon him.

The engine struck. The trike shot ahead. It left the rails, turned over in the middle with Tim entangled. Again the engine struck, hurling it on to a culvert where it hammed between the transomes. And struck again and smashed the thing to pieces and thundered over and away. Slowly Tim's broken body freed itself and slid through the transomes, fell into a little creek below, crumpled and dead among the scattered presents, its warm blood trickling into the tinkling stream. Oh, death of a kangaroo for a Sergeant Major![28]

It is possible, I suppose, to argue that Tim's death is due to human error—that of his drunken comrades. (It would be a hard critic who argued that it is due to his own preoccupation with his loved ones and his resulting negligence.) To a certain extent this is true, but it is much more to the point, I think, to consider where Herbert places his whole emotional stress in the description of the incident. Continually the weight of the prose falls on the essential goodness of Tim and on the relationship of that goodness to his disastrous fate. Strident and absurd militarist though he is, he is constantly shown as one of only a tiny handful of characters who behave with decency towards blacks in the novel.

In the passage quoted, as well as frequently prior to it, Herbert pointedly contrasts Tim's sobriety with the drunken helplessness of the rest of the gangers: they are incapable even of receiving his Christmas greetings. Everything that can possibly contribute to the irony of the situation and its basic injustice is seized upon by the author and played up for all its worth. The doomed man thinks of nothing but the loving reception awaiting him at home. He is Father Christmas. At precisely the point where the train appears Tim is thinking scornfully of the limited powers of his colleagues of hearing trains on the line, as compared to those of his foster daughter Tocky. But the key sentence of all is undoubtedly the brief statement that "His foot caught in the load of love." Not merely his thoughts of his family but even the actual physical products of his love for them become the instruments of his downfall.

As with Peter Differ, the death of the leader of the clan produces its immediate collapse. Following this passage describing Tim's death, Herbert spends only a brief half page outlining the whole collapse of Tim's fragile military garrison. The distance of the author from the characters, and the pointedness with which he picks up any ironic possibilities inherent in the situation and exploits them is more suggestive than anything else of the relative inability of man to control his own fate. The comparatively decent impulses in the novel (which are comparatively few) are just as ineffectual and doomed to failure as the many criminal ones. One could go further and say, without denigration of the novel, that its interest in moral and psychological complexity is minimal and that its author's powers of characterization are crude and limited.

V   Herbert's Psychological Characterization

Harry Heseltine has suggested, in his Oxford series pamphlet on Xavier Herbert, that Capricornia was invented "for the primary imaginative purpose of coming to grips with his (Herbert's) own ambiguous attitudes towards his father,"[29] and the author himself would almost certainly subscribe to that suggestion. In *Disturbing Element* we saw that he spoke continually of his hurt and disappointment—and consequently, his near emasculation—at his father's rejection of him; and the hero of *Poor Fellow My Country*, Jeremy

Delacy, is continually spoken of as arousing other characters' love
through their seeing him in a quasipaternal role, "father and lover
combined to perfection in the one man."[30] Love in Herbert's novels
is associated in a continual and somewhat reductive way with need,
or even weakness, sometimes to the point of being equated with
those qualities.

But if the preoccupation with father figures is present in his
fiction it is so in a fairly crude and mechanistic way. In the case of
Capricornia, the suggestion seems to me to be incorrect even on a
quite simple factual level. Norman does not spend his time worrying
about his father. He accepts Oscar quite easily when he discovers
that he is not his true father: "Steady Dad. I'm not upset. Not a bit.
Don't get yourself worked up. I know all about him. He's not a bad
sort. But he means nothing to me. You're my Dad, you know—my
dear old Dad."[31] Later, after Oscar dies, he becomes friendly to
Mark and shown no signs of traumas in regard to his true father. His
dilemma is not with his father but with his identity as a half-caste in
a society which despises such. Like Huck Finn, he is ashamed of his
best impulses and except for a few moments, such as after Andy
McRandy's impassioned speech on behalf of the Binghis or during
his own outburst in court, he remains persuaded by society's
prejudices that those better impulses are wrong.

But there is a more fundamental objection, I think, to the kind of
argument that reads the novel in this Freudian way. Whatever
Herbert's own belief or intention, the whole mode of the novel and
in particular the extent to which the authorial consciousness stands
aloof from all of the characters not merely facilitates its satiric
function of attacking the treatment of the Aborigines but also
necessarily precludes any deep psychological involvement or analysis. Characters brawl, indulge in Black Velvet, drink enormous
quantities of beer, but the sense of a deep inner life is absent; we
are a long way here from the Jamesian world of subtle psychological
perceptions and discriminations of motive and conduct.

It is particularly noticeable how many times and with what degree
of explicitness Herbert will intervene directly in the narrative to
guide our responses. He does this by the satiric tags he appends to
the white race, the "Masters of Mankind" and "the Great White
Peoples," and their corresponding view of the Aborigines as "the
Ragtag of Humanity." The irony here is distinguished far more by
its robustness than by its subtlety. The author feels free to comment
openly on the foibles and follies of the whites, as when he points to

the courses of action Jock Driver offers the natives, who "would be put the alternatives of starving or eating Jock's cattle or going to work for him. The second would be their choice till the police came and shot them . . . And all the while the Nation was boasting to the world of its Freedom and Manliness and Honesty. Australia Felix!"[32]

This hortatory element is never far from Herbert's prose and particularly likely to make itself present in authorial generalizations. What stops the novel from becoming excessively garrulous and didactic is firstly that Herbert does not, for the most part, extend his moralizing very far towards individual characters: it is almost as if his belief in the possibilities of human virtue is so limited that he sees little point in criticizing its absence. And secondly, that his imaginative energies are so engaged by the world of Capricornia that he is more fascinated by its anarchic energy than he is appalled by its disgraceful injustices. The same direct intervention occurs when he observes a group of fifty passengers, due to leave for the South, disappear for a last indulgence in Black Velvet. "Those lusty fellows, product of two thousand years of Constituted Authority and Christian Virtue,"[33] he says of them almost genially, as if his fascination with their excesses has overcome his outraged contempt for them.

But the author reveals his own thoughts most fully in two set scenes which are given great weight in the novel. The first is the argument between Oscar and Peter Differ concerning the future of the young half-caste Naw-nim.[34] It is a long and eloquent speech by Differ, punctuated only by angry objections from Oscar, in which he makes a passionate plea for the fair treatment of Aborigines and half-castes and recognition of their innate capacity to lead productive lives if given the chance. The distinction between author and character at this point is so minimal as to be almost nonexistent, a fact which is emphasized by the almost complete absence of expository prose accompanying the dialogue of the two men. Differ's sanity and wisdom are placed in a tragic light by Oscar's refusal to listen to him and his brutal neglect of both Differ and his daughter Connie as he is dying.

A similar scene occurs much later in the novel, when a long speech from the character known as Andy McRandy focuses on two of the major issues of the novel—the land of Capricornia and its potential that is being so tragically squandered by its inhabitants, and the problem of Norman's ambiguous identity (his name derives from the Aboriginal "Naw-nim", meaning "no name"). On both,

Herbert's feelings are clearly ambivalent. Andy tells Norman, "We're a great people, we Australians. There's nuthin' to touch us in the world"[35] and in a peculiar way I think that Herbert is not being wholly ironical, that he offers a certain limited endorsement of this view—at least insofar as it represents an aspiration rather than an achievement. The period of optimism in Australian literature is very brief indeed, and even then not shared by most of the best writers. Later writers, such as Patrick White and A. D. Hope, as well of course as the later Herbert himself, have a distinctly pessimistic view which is epitomized in the title of Herbert's last novel. But one of the most painful elements in *Capricornia* is the sense of a tragically squandered opportunity to create a paradise— or more accurately, the sense of the destruction of the paradise that was already there before the coming of the dingo. As Andy puts it, in urging Norman to acknowledge and not betray his origins, "What is the perfect state of society? Aint it the one in which everyone's equally happy and well fed? If it is, then Brother Binghi has it."[36]

Andy's long speech is the most eloquent and openly affirmative gesture in the book and even here Herbert quickly reverts to his more usual robust irony with the statement that "Norman remained proud of his Aboriginal heritage for several weeks."[37] I referred earlier to the crudity and explicitness of some of Herbert's irony, which sometimes more resembles haranguing sarcasm, but in dealing with Norman he is at his most restrained and effective. And the irony is made all the more poignant by the fact that Herbert points without overt comment to the most painful element in it of all— that so entrenched in white attitudes is Norman himself that he is unable to follow the wise advice of Andy and be proud of his heritage, rather than conforming to other people's prejudices and attempting to reject it.

Significantly his only true moment of deep understanding in the novel comes when he goes " walkabout"—that is, journeys into the bush—from his father's home and hears the Song of the Golden Beetle:

Soon he forgot his debasement. And he found himself marvelling at the phenomenon of his existence as a creature, of the existence of Mankind, and of nature's contrariety to Man that made Man's ingenuity essential. And for the first time in his life he began consciously to doubt the existence of the conventional Divinity in which he had been trained to believe, and to wonder about the Something he could see in the stars. So he came to marvel at Infinity instead of fearing it.[38]

For the first time Norman responds to what Herbert frequently apostrophizes as "The Spirit of the Land"—in deep contrast to the whites who merely ravage and despoil it. But the tragedy is that he soon turns his back on that experience and denies even that he went walkabout but was merely trapped by the floods. (Herbert seems to suggest that his claim may have been true although Andy and the others clearly don't believe it, but in any event that is beside the point: the essential thing is that Norman is ashamed of the imputation that he should follow any black custom.)

The ironic mode of the novel, then, all pervasive except for the two set speeches mentioned earlier and for rare bursts of eloquence associated with the blacks to be discussed shortly is by and large one that precludes treatment of characters in psychological depth; the novel is not primarily concerned with investigation and analysis of personality. It is also a mode that works from an enormous authorial distance. *Capricornia* has often been compared to an earlier classic Australian novel, Joseph Furphy's *Such is Life,* with which it shares something of the same intuitive radicalism of form beneath an apparently aimless organization. The differences between the two novels, however, are even more striking than the similarities, notably in their fundamentally opposed manner of narration. The first-person, anecdotal nature of *Such is Life* restricts a large part of the consciousness of the protagonists to the central character; the conscious detachment of the narrator in *Capricornia* on the other hand, Fielding-like in his intrusion into the narrative in order to remind us of his apartness from it, means that the extent to which all human consciousness can be rendered or explored is extremely limited. What both novels have in common, then, although they arrive at it by opposed means, is an absence of the kind of concern that was supposed to be the business of novels, at least until fairly recently.

An examination of even the most fully rendered of the characters in *Capricornia*—Norman obviously, Mark and Oscar, Tocky, Tim O'Cannon—quickly suggests the limitations of their complexity and individuality. Even when Herbert makes one of his rare attempts at this kind of writing he is able to achieve only dramatically crude notation, observing the workings of the character's imagination from outside rather than dramatizing the processes of his consciousness. A good example is Norman's submission to the Song of the Golden Beetle, which is seen as a purely external, almost metaphysical force. The imaginative element in Norman—considerably greater than that of most of the other protagonists—cannot be directly evoked or rendered but must be observed by a kind of external correlative, the summoning up of the mysterious forces of nature apart from the character, to which he dimly responds as he becomes aware of them.

Of course, the Golden Beetle passages have a further significance in that they represent one of several attempts in the novel to juxtapose against the anarchism of the whites a kind of lyrical affirmation of nature that is associated with the Aborigines. As The Shouter in court says of his client Norman, ". . .he was written what he calls poetry, reads a great deal, spends most of his time dreaming. This is Aboriginal," he adds for the benefit of the court,[39] with the implication that it is therefore to be excused. But as Beverley Hahn has pointed out, in an unpublished paper on *Capricornia*, these lyrical, natural impulses represented by the Aboriginals cannot even sustain themselves, let alone overcome the forces of white rapacity and commercialism. The following description of dawn rising has something of the same quality of the false dawn which failed to satisfy the expectations of the English people in *A Passage to India*:

Two black birds flapped slowly out to meet the day; and as though their going had to do with it, a golden glow swelled in the east, swelled, swelled, appearing like the halo of a mighty Christ—and Oh! the golden sun burst forth and touched the prostrate earth with trembling fingers, touched the hoary head of Tim and blessed him. But just as golden Youth from gentleness to harshness turns, so did the infant sun spring up and sweep the sentimental worshipping world with harsh white cynical light and bleach it, bleach it of the gentle-tinted humbugs that, by eventide, itself would have adopted, and left it stark, bewildered, and distressed.[40]

Tim is one of the few characters who has something of the Aboriginal response to the pastoral, and it is strikingly significant that almost immediately after this passage the scene, quoted earlier, of his being killed by the train takes place. Generally speaking, as the novel goes on, the lyrical impulse tends to disappear to be engulfed by the rapacious and commercially successful character of The Shouter. Similarly, the Aboriginal elements in Norman become more and more quiescent and at the end we see him happily planning to make himself rich again, with his father and Heather. while the tragic figure of Tocky is neglected and forgotten.

There is a further method by which the author attempts a kind of characterization, one that has led him to be compared frequently with Dickens, and that is his use of metaphor. Tim O'Cannon, for instance, is in some respects a strikingly Dickensian figure translated into an Australian setting. An even more conspicuous example is the character of The Shouter, who dominates the later pages of the novel to a sometimes tedious extent. Like many of Dickens's characters, he is seen partly in the form of his resemblance to animals. But there is nothing of the brilliance of the metaphor, say, in *Hard Times*, of "a melancholy elephant in a state of madness." The metaphors tend, in fact, not to be metaphors at all but merely lists. In comparison with Dickens, the imagery is mechanical, with Norman merely picturing The Shouter as an almost endless succession of birds and animals—elephant, crab, bull, lamb, toad, dove, turkey-cock, shark, spider, crocodile, ass, angel-fish, stingaree, buffalo-bull, python, octopus, camel, eagle, purring cat, until the very profusion of creatures ends up destroying the original effect.

The measure of the limits of psychological depth can be seen in the fact that, generally speaking, most of the characters can affect us to varying but limited degrees which are measurable largely in terms of their situation, rather than through any intrinsic growth or discovery of consciousness they may achieve. Tocky starving miserably to death in a rain tank, Tim O'Cannon being struck down by a train on Christmas morning as he travels home with his gifts. . .these poignant and moving incidents are so by virtue of their intrinsically tragic nature, not primarily by virtue of how well we have come to know or identify with the characters themselves. They remain demonstrations of the intrinsic anarchy of the world of Capricornia and the impotence of its inhabitants, their inability to control their own destinies. We extend sympathy and compassion, but from a standpoint "above" the characters, not as identifying closely with them.

Sometimes, moreover, the authorial aloofness is so great as to make even quite harrowing incidents a source of comedy. The murder of the native by Krater in chapter four, for example, is described in terms that emphasize the incongruity between the desperate act and Krater's matter of fact expectations of the native's cooperation: " 'I'm only puttin' y' outer mis'ry, me lad,' gasped Krater. 'Gawd-sake keep still.' "[41] This disorienting approach makes it impossible for the reader to view the struggle in terms of conventional sympathy alone, or even to respond to its tension and suspense as narrative, but instead gives it a comically incongruous effect.

The deaths of Joe Ballest and Mick O'Pick, similarly, are appalling in one sense; but overriding this whole section are both Herbert's structural ironies (Joe hurls himself against a train, believing Mick is dead; Mick turns up alive, but then he himself is killed four days later) and the basic absurdity of their brawling. Even in the midst of their slapstick fight, very comically described, Herbert coldly points out that "Both old fools were always in dead earnest."[42] It is this detachment, perhaps, more than anything else that has led one critic to go so far as to suggest that, with two or three exceptions, we actually "enjoy" the deaths in the novel.

Finally, it is noticeable that except for a few impassioned speeches, notably those of Differ's cited, McRandy's concerning the blacks, and Norman's denunciation of the whites in court, the characters are largely inarticulate, lacking in introspection, a further factor inhibiting a treatment that would place stress on psychological depth. Even their actions are limited mostly to the physical—drinking, brawling after indulging in drink, Black Velvet—and are repeated so often throughout the novel that they assume by the end of it an almost ritualistic quality.

VI *The Design of* Capricornia

It is not individual characters, then, but the whole pattern of the world of *Capricornia* that we are primarily asked to pay attention to. It is the design of the novel, a design which is essentially structural and in which characterization, limited and subordinate, plays one part only. The author's distanced, omniscient point of view and the considerable liberties he obviously feels himself entitled to take in directing the reader's attention to the points he wants to make are ideally suited to directing him away from the particular and the inner, towards the overall and the exterior. Herbert points constantly to the facts of anomaly and anarchism in the world of the Capricornians yet at the same time expresses in his repeated ironies and the glee with which he documents them an exuberant vitalism which is oddly at war with the novel's pessimism and fatalism. This vision is not present merely in individual generalizations but pervades the whole structure of the novel. It does this particularly in three ways.

The first is in comparison between individual characters. Norman's peculiar position as a half-caste (yet one brought up as a white man) allows him to become a focal point of comparisons with several other characters whose situation is a variation on his. I mentioned earlier the fact of Oscar's eventual, reluctant acceptance of his nephew and rejection of Connie Differ, two choices which, with their consequences, are counterpointed throughout the entire novel in the eventual fates of Connie and her daughter Tocky. Not only is Tocky's story juxtaposed against that of Norman, but in the latter stages of the book, so is Charlie Ket's as well. He, too, is a half-caste who, in the early stages of his appearance attempts, like Norman, to claim a distinguished ancestry for himself, and is exposed. He tries to treat Norman as an equal, as half-castes do throughout the novel, and with the other half-castes is rebuffed every time. He has a history of violence which resembles that of another half-caste Yeller Elbert and although hardly the most attractive of characters many of his defects of personality can be attributed largely to the unjust manner in which he has been treated.

Because of the presence of the blacks, and the way in which they are regarded by the whites, *Capricornia* is probably more about class and class distinctions and snobberies, oddly enough, than almost any other Australian novel, and the discriminations, for all that they are sometimes crudely expressed, are sometimes as narrow and acute as in a Jane Austen novel. Witness, for instance, the reasons given by the various characters for Oscar's dismissing most of his workmen when Norman comes to be employed in his ranch. Charles Ket, as he insists on being called, Norman himself, and Frank McLash all interpret his motives in different ways, with only Frank grasping the real reason—that Oscar has carefully judged who would find Norman acceptable and who would not. Or similarly, there is Marigold's dilemma that she genuinely loves Norman but cannot overcome her fear of societal disapproval to allow him to embrace her publicly. Or there is Norman's eventual seeing the light in which he is truly regarded when he attempts to kiss Rhoda and the company's fragile pretense that he is equal abruptly disintegrates.

Only in one stunning image do black and white finally come together, and this is in the scene in which Krater and a native are dying but the white man insists on their both making a last, determined effort to find assistance. In the grimmest image in the novel of black and white uniting, Herbert writes laconically:

A thousand flies went with them to suck their suppurating sores. Time and again they fell by the way exhausted, and would have died there but for Krater's Anglo-Saxon will, which could not realise that it was inextricably in the grip of death and hence flogged the wretched body on to unnecessary misery. On they went and on and on, Stone-Age Man and Anglo-Saxon, clinging to each other for support, blending the matter of their sores.[43]

There are other comparisons of characters—Mark and Oscar Shillingsworth are two sides of the same coin, for instance—but even more pervasive are the pointed juxtapositions of events simultaneous in time that occur throughout the novel. Most of these are based around the double standard of morality exercised through the novel by Capricornians when they deal with blacks and whites. For instance, fairly early in the novel Herbert points to "a gang of black felons working on the road and . . . a gang of white ones fishing from the cliff,"[44] although on this occasion he makes no comment. Much more overt is the series of deliberate parallels he sets up later in the novel in dealing with Tocky O'Cannon and her sojourn in the Compound. Tocky is recalled to her drudgery by "a burst of laughter" from the nurses' quarters. The black servants and temporary workers are paid nothing for their work; in fact, Herbert points to the fact that Dr. Aintee's salary "amounted to about a quarter of the total expenditure on Aboriginal Affairs in Capricornia."[45] The white sisters prove to be far more amorous than the black waifs whose morals they guard so jealously. As the whites leave after castigating the natives, a crowd arrives to persuade them to do exactly what the blacks had done and have a midnight picnic. As they leave, "squealing and yelling like children," "A child in the Home began to wail. Then another wailed, another."[46] The juxtaposition could not be more pointed. Herbert points again and again to ironies and anomalies such as these—the salary of the Resident commissioner, for instance, being more than the amount of money paid for the upkeep of all the natives in the Compound, or the size of the half-castes' home being equal to that of the matron.

Finally, there are the repeated actions—deaths, funerals, fights, accidents (especially those involving the train), nomadic wanderings, trials in court—that form the fabric of the book and are placed in implicit comparison with one another. As Brian Kiernan has pointed out:

The coincidences function in a way that Dickens' often do—to suggest that the characters represent as a microcosm the society implied beyond them: that their interactions, "unrealistic" as they may at times appear, reveal at a deeper and more general level the nature of social relationships.[47]

Both as fact and symbol, the destructiveness and the failure to expand of the railway is crucial to the book's moral design.

In all these structural patterns Herbert is exerting a shaping control over a narrative that is only superficially sprawling and untidy. *Capricornia,* masterpiece that it is, is a novel designed to make us think as well as feel, and the kind of limits of characterization that in a more conventional novelist would have spelled failure are here triumphantly exploited.

Without wishing for a moment to discount the tone of passionate protest that marks Herbert's treatment of white injustices inflicted on blacks, it seems to me crucially important to note also that the final effect of the novel far transcends the mere propaganda that forms its worst parts. In its originality of form, in the extraordinary richness and inventiveness with which the author has created his world of Capricornia, and in the robust and exuberant vitality with which he responds to it, it seems to me to be an achievement unique in Australian fiction.

CHAPTER 3

Seven Emus

THE heart of Xavier Herbert's achievement lies in the three long
novels he wrote, over the space of something like forty years and
at widely separated intervals. In between, however, he has published three shorter works which, if they do not pretend to the
ambition of the major works, have a more than biographical interest.
Curiously enough, all three appeared in the five years of furious
activity between 1959 and 1963 that also included the second long
novel, *Soldiers' Women*. The first, and least interesting of these is
Seven Emus, a distinctly minor yarn, in the tradition of the tall story
familiar to American readers of Bret Harte and Mark Twain and
Australian readers of Henry Lawson and many other writers of
exaggerated jokes. I mentioned in an earlier chapter the unusual
circumstances surrounding its publication, which Herbert explains
in his article "I Sinned Against Syntax." There is perhaps one
further point Herbert makes in the article which is worthy of
mention.

He complains that although *Capricornia* enjoyed considerable
financial success it failed to receive the plaudits of the literary
establishment. This claim is at least dubious. As I pointed out
earlier, it received very good reviews at the time of its publication
(the maligned "Inky" Stephensen being particularly generous in his
Publicist) and the admittedly scant attention it has received to date
in critical journals has all been laudatory. It is also taught in virtually
all courses in Australian literature in this country. What is important,
though, is that one of Herbert's animating motives behind writing
the book is that he wished to write a novel so markedly and
obviously original and innovative that critics could not possibly
ignore it or suggest that it came about by accident. The tension
Herbert feels towards the academic establishment—a tension often
found in self-taught men—is evident in both the motives he gives

67

for writing the book and in his contemptuous attitude towards academics in the text of the novel itself.

Thematically, the novel holds some interest for the reader of Herbert's work and according to the author himself it played a very necessary therapeutic role in freeing his own creative energies for larger and more ambitious projects. For these reasons it has some value. In its own right, however, it is a very minor and feeble work which, as Herbert says in tones of ambivalence, critics were not slow to point out. In the *Meanjin* article mentioned earlier he writes:

> Those reviews!
>
> *Seven Emus* was condemned for not being the masterpiece that erstwhile botch *Capricornia* had become in the meantime. But that did not worry me, since I was conceded a masterpiece at least in the past. What I wanted to know was how they liked 'the style'. Lord, how they *did not* like it; how they howled over my curly clevernesses as affectations; how they counted the words between my full stops, charged me with having no idea of literary construction, with writing sentences to fill whole pages!
>
> Actually my sentences were not unduly long, and were more markedly divided than by the conventional method, because *two* stops were used instead of one. My own precious syntactical system demanded that a paragraph consist of an entity of the whole composition that was self-contained and hence could have but one initial capital and one concluding stop. Pauses between parts of this entity, which conventionally would be marked with a full stop, were marked with two points, thus .. I believe that by my system emotion could be better expressed than with the conventional, which would demand conventional reading.
>
> Not that I am defending myself. Heavens, no! I have been publicly stoned for sinning against established syntax, and I am truly contrite.[1]

The uneasy tone here—a curious mixture of aggressive resentment toward his critics and a kind of grudging admission that they might be right— helps to conceal the real point, which is that *Seven Emus* is the least considerable and successful book he has written, and the reasons for that have little or nothing to do with its so-called "style." Whether it used one full stop or ten would make no difference. As the author admits in the same article, "*Seven Emus* was quite a small thing, actually built out of an idea for a mere short story"[2] and to pad it out to even the relatively small length of one hundred and forty-seven generously spaced pages required the insertion of a good deal of superfluous material. In the case of *Seven Emus*, this consists of repetition at tedious length, long didactic passages in which the authorial intrusion is blatant, prolix and distracting, and the energetic riding of many of Herbert's familiar hobby-horses, ranging from the self-interest and careerism of academics, through whites' mistreatment of Aboriginals and the inequity of the law courts to sneers at the folly of pure rationalism, which the author repeatedly signifies as "the scientific method."

The actual method of using two successive full stops is something of a red herring one hardly notices after a few pages. Herbert's mistake was to imagine that true originality could be brought about by artificial means such as changing a method of punctuation. The only important critical question is whether Herbert's preoccupation with his new system was partly responsible for what is the book's other chief characteristic, its tediously involuted and circumlocutory prose style, sentences marked by Faulknerian length and indirection but without Faulknerian complexity.

I   *Structure and Authorial Distance*

Seven Emus is the name of a cattle-run in the Northwest of Australia, near a township identified only by the fictitious name of Dampier. Prior to the action of the story beginning, it had been wholly owned by half-caste Bronco Jones, but he has just been tricked into giving over half of it to a plausible rogue named Appleby Gaunt, whose self-styled title is "Baron." To Dampier there comes an academic interested in anthropology and self-promotion, "Mr. Malcolm Goborrow, B.A., Dip. Anth." (Herbert's penchant for figurative names is again present in this novel.) Goborrow discovers a precious Aboriginal artifact, the dreaming-stone of the now lost Emu tribe, inside a cave that was a sacred place, and with the cooperation of the Baron attempts by a ruse to steal it away from its rightful owners. How the two men at first appear to be successful and Bronco to suffer from the loss of the good luck charm until the last few pages, when his luck changes and fate works ironically to thwart the two white thieves, is really all the substance there is to the story.

Seven Emus is fairly slow to get under way. The first five chapters, consisting of thirty pages, are all a part of a build-up to the actual sequence of events with which the novella is concerned, commencing with the arrival of Goborrow at the cattle-run. They are a preliminary and somewhat long-winded prelude to an understanding of the action.

Herbert's narrative stance throughout these and the later pages is

again one of careful and conscious distancing from the action. It is
established in the brooding ominousness with which the arrival of
Goborrow is described—"Thus that stranger, whose coming on the
day at which this tale begins set off the train of events culminating
in the crisis which decided the fate of the station"[3]—and continues
with, for example, his description of the two swindlers' approach to
the cave:

but even in celerity they were unfortunate, for had they taken half an hour
longer, even a little less than that, the circumstances that joined with the
primary unscientific neglect of a degree of direction and half a mile of
distance to spell misfortune would not have continued to exist. . .[4]

He is similarly aloof, as he was in *Capricornia,* in pointing to the
pattern of misunderstandings that continues throughout the tale,
though these often represent deliberate acts of duplicity, rather than
the workings of a malign fate. He points very coldly, for instance, to
the fact that Bronco's sons leave off their eavesdropping too soon
and fail to hear something that might have made their discomfort
worthwhile. Bronco himself is taken in very easily by the wild
schemes of both tricksters in turn—the Baron's model windmill and
Goborrow's fantastic scheme for the Euraustralian League—and it
is even hinted that it is the white blood in him, with its propensity
to avarice, that gets him entangled with the Baron in the first place.
The two thieves themselves, of course, act with duplicity throughout
the entire story, concocting one false scheme after another and
never trusting even one another.

Herbert distances himself further by the assumption of authorial
omniscience that he makes very early in the novel. Speaking of how
much Goborrow already knew about the Baron before meeting him,
he adds, ". . . but it matters little whether he had the facts or not,
since we have them."[5] But he is curiously uncertain in this stance
and only a few pages later comments:

As we have said that for aught anyone knew of the truth concerning the
antecedents of Appleby Gaunt, our Baron, these same were anyone's guess,
let us hazard a bit of guessing, without pretending to discover anything like
the facts about him, which would be soothsaying, but simply to make
deductions on the much that was unknown about him from the little that
was known, with fair certainty of getting enough evidence for our purpose,
which is to establish some sort of understanding of the man so as to

appreciate as fully as possible his behaviour in the peculiar situation he was
involved in according to this tale.[6]

The above sentence would be a fair and representative example
of both the author's uncertainty as to what kind of approach to
bring to his material and the prolixity of much of his prose. One
attempt at resolving the former problem seems to be, as Heseltine
has pointed out, the hinting of the story as being a kind of fairy tale.
The opening chapter, with its sympathetic and well-informed
account of the Aboriginal legends, is imbued with a fable-like
atmosphere and deals with "Dream-time Heroes." In a discussion
of the Baron's character in chapter three Herbert speaks of "the
inexorable dragon of reality" rising up "to destroy his dream-
castles,"[7] and such language from the world of fairy tales is not
uncommon. The cave with its hidden treasure—the precious To-
tem—is a familiar element from the same world and Bronco is
spoken of as being fanatical about it: "He guards that cave like a
dragon."[8] Even the unexpected happy ending is part of the same
element while the Baron's proposed book is spoken of as having "a
subtle element of fairy-tale success in it."[9]

Such a mode, however, requires a lightness of touch which this
book is far from possessing. Continually Herbert intrudes to direct
his readers' responses in a heavyhanded way. The novel is filled
with passages in which the author's concerns are not so much
dramatized as merely asserted, often with considerable repetition.
While most of the views he puts forward are perfectly unexception-
able and at best—as in his pervasive sympathy for the blacks and
their traditions—wholly admirable, they remain only that—views,
opinions, not rendered experience.

Herbert rails at the squatter who buys a knighthood, at the type
of academic of whom we are given one cliched representative, at
psychoanalysis (while himself indulging in it in crude form), at
whites' treatment of blacks, at what he calls "the scientific method"
which he mentions in various forms at least half a dozen times, at
the inequities of the law, and at intellectuality and at intellectuals
(not always the same thing as academics) in general. Typical of his
bludgeoning treatment of his characters at its worst is this description of the two swindlers approaching the cave:

. . . young men like this one now whimpering in petty rage at prospect of
being benighted within ace of accomplishment of his knavery, who had
never been initiated into anything at all, whose only cult was self-seeking,

whose conception of manhood was bluff and bully and cuddle up in the soft
comforts of women's company .. whimpering, while his elder, so far from
being a watcher over the virtue of the young, was moaning that he could no
longer see, whining that he feared to break a leg, snivelling that he could
not go another step.[10]

It is probably due to frankly contemptuous language such as this
in which the two men are described, as much as the overall
slightness of the tale, that the characters achieve so little psychological depth or richness. Although each of the three main characters is
given an entire chapter early in the tale, generally speaking they
remain little more than pale stereotypes.

At first, Herbert does seem to have a genuine interest in the
Baron. The swindler has always been a type that interests him—one
thinks of The Shouter in *Capricornia* and the odd mixture of
qualities he is depicted as possessing—and early in the novel the
author's attitude towards the Baron is one of almost Jonsonian
benignity as one almost disinterested in his profession: "Your true
rogue is interested in gain less than in the practice of roguery, a fact
self-evident, since gain would be easier and greater got by a
conventional application of the sharp intelligence needful in a
rogue."[11] Subsequent facts do not bear out this genial view,
unfortunately, and Herbert's tone becomes noticeably sterner as
Gaunt's activities are revealed. There is also a very crudely specula-
tive attempt to explain him in psychoanalytic terms as mother
dominated, the psychological phenomenon to which Herbert returns
so often, and at another point the names Freud and Malinowski are
invoked in a rather unexpected context.

Goborrow is, as I mentioned earlier, the stereotype of the go-
getting academic who abuses Herbert's beloved discipline of anthropology (Herbert once had dreams of acquiring qualifications in the
subject himself and at the beginning of chapter five there is a kind
of hymn to anthropology). He is filled out only in terms of a number
of repeated tags—"the Golden Girl," his dream of a chairmanship,
and so on—that convey little sense of an individual character.

Bronco, the most interesting of the three, is given a little more
substance but once again Herbert tends to resort (as he was later to
do in *Poor Fellow My Country*) to simple, repeated gestures, such
as his face working with emotion, to give us a sense of the character.
But Bronco is, finally, the most complex figure and the most central
to the novel's concerns.

II   *The Problem of the Half-Caste*

As a half-caste (or more accurately, quarter-caste) Bronco is in a curiously ambiguous position in the world of the novel. To the two old black men Moonduk and Mardoo he is an outsider, despite his attempts to protect the Dreaming-Stone. They address him as "you-feller," coupling him with the two white men, and it is perhaps significant that he is taken in by the spurious Dreaming-Stone, just as Goborrow himself was. Both Goborrow and the Baron claim to regard him as a white man, of course, especially when it suits their purpose, and they exploit his own feelings of ambivalence, especially in their creation of the Euraustralian League, while behind his back dismissing him contemptuously as a primitive. Like Norman-Nawnim in *Capricornia* he is caught between two worlds, belonging wholly to neither, and the same ambiguous position he is granted on the cattle-run repeats itself in his visit to the city.

There, his attempts to form a group of natives interested in the Euraustralian League are notably unsuccessful until he backs them up with a nine gallon keg of beer (recalling the wedding in *Capricornia* when Tim O'Cannon received three hundred and seventeen replies to his one hundred and eighteen invitations after announcing that he would be supplying four hundred and twenty gallons of beer). A brawl ensues, and in consequence Bronco is thrown into jail and given the usual unjust trial that awaits suspected black malefactors in Herbert's novels: his experiences of defending Aborigines in court have clearly formed Herbert's views of the operations of justice, which are as scathing as those of Dickens. Later, again, Bronco is thrown out of the Hotel Timor, which is segregated: "The hard eyes of the barman were on Bronco, who met them, read them, and drooping turned and slunk outside."[12]

At the same time, and although Herbert is frequently and bluntly satirical at the expense of the whites in their treatment of the Aborigines, he shows Bronco winning a certain measure of respect among the whites of the town. The bank is prepared to back him if he can get rid of his white partner, an unexpectedly ironical reversal of affairs, and Mr. Knowell, the lawyer, also comes belatedly to his defence. The squatter Poundamore is an unusually benevolent portrayal of the type in Herbert's fiction; and if Herbert still sneers at the whites' betrayal of the Aborigines' heritage, speaking of "these days of dawning national conscience concerning the long-standing disregard of the rights of Aborigines"[13] at least he admits that there has been some improvement in the area—one to which he himself has contributed in no small measure.

One further possible suggestion — that Herbert's presentation of the ambiguous position of half-castes in the Northern community was a reflection of his own relationship with his parents—is, I think, mistaken. I have argued before that despite the author's preoccupation with themes of parental domination — a preoccupation *stated* more than rendered artistically — his work is never marked by deep complexity of consciousness; he remains too far outside the consciousness of his characters, too determinedly aloof, to give us more than a rudimentary sense of how their minds and souls are working. In *Seven Emus,* more even than in any of the other novels, the characters are little more than ciphers, sketched only in broad outline.

The truth is that relationships between blacks and whites have always been at the heart of Herbert's work, except for *Soldiers' Women,* and the half- or quarter-caste is the figure who most dramatically embodies the tensions between the two groups. *Seven Emus* is a satirical expression of the author's pessimism concerning the future of Aborigines and part-Aborigines in Australia; the "Euraustralian League" is the target for his crudest and most vehement satire. Speaking of his attempts to find a solution to the black problem in Australia, Herbert wrote:

I did not know for a long while that what was wrong was that I knew, but would not admit, that *there is no solution to the problem, at least no practical one.*

I made the admission at last, tacitly, in "Seven Emus", which shows full bloods for what they are, a people doomed to non-progress, the poorest of poor who will be with us always, the "boongs" and "stinkers", to whose similarly doomed children not only the whites of Elliot object as fit associates for their own, but also their half-brethren, those people of the new race, Euraustralians (or cross-breeds).[14]

Although *Seven Emus* ends happily, as a fairy tale should, its presentation of the dilemmas of the blacks in general is a pessimistic one and the strain of Herbert's struggle to retain artistic composure is evident throughout the work.

III   *The Spirit of the Land*

One aspect of the fundamental difference between the two races, and one which Herbert insists on again and again, will be familiar to readers of his other books. It is his belief that the natives have a deep spiritual accord with the land of their birth, whereas the whites are mere transient intruders upon it. The contrast is drawn right throughout the novel but appears at fullest length in an important passage that sums up much of the peculiar nature of Herbert's nationalism.

> The spirit of a place is emanation of the history of the place created in the minds of men .. and the only history hereabout was the ancient black man's, enough of these modern white men knew to create the spirit of the place for themselves, or rather to have it created involuntarily within them, since it is a natural human faculty so to do, man being first of the earth earthy and ever wanting oneness with his physical surroundings, hence the phenomenon of patriotism, so strong in the savage because he has created the history of his country to suit the spirit he has already imagined for it, so weak in colonials like the white Australians, like this pair, who have to live unsatisfied of soul because acceptance of the spirit of the land of their origin is denied them who are born alien to that land, and they cannot create any worth while spirit out of history as little as their own, nor out of the rich history of their black compatriots because that would be beneath their dignity .. and they are for ever at a loss, not understanding that such things are of the soul, not of the mind, that there is no logic in them, only the psychic satisfaction that is the stuff other than bread by which men live.[15]

The "spirit of the land" is, of course, a phrase that occurs repeatedly in Herbert's writing and this passage is merely the most extended drawing of a series of contrasts between the blacks like Moonduc and Mardoo who, for all their comic appurtenances, are figures of genuine dignity and spiritual depth, and the white marauders like Goborrow especially, whose pretensions via anthropological study to some understanding of Aboriginal culture and custom are mercilessly mocked. Similarly, the dichotomy here drawn between "mind" and "soul"—between, in other words, the purely cerebral, "scientific method" on the one hand and genuine spiritual feeling on the other—is crucial to the whole novel.

Bronco, a pivotal figure in this, is shown several times as being torn between his "black" and "white" feelings. Herbert notes of him at one point, ".. at any rate, it was Bronco's yielding to his complex white man's urge to combine business with pleasure that ruined the arcadian existence to which the simpler part of his nature inclined."[16] Similarly, the Baron says contemptuously of Bronco, "It's the black fellow in him, I suppose. He's got to have something to believe in."[17] Continually, from the opening chapter, the Aborigines' beliefs are described in the only fine language the novel has to

show, with the emphasis on the antiquity and unbroken continuity
of the land and their feeling for it. It is a feeling to which, for all his
professed anthropological learning, Goborrow with his crassly materialistic and rationalistic nature is totally impervious.

IV   *Conclusion*

Thematically, then, *Seven Emus* is a not unimportant work in that
it embodies many of Herbert's characteristic preoccupations. The
series of tensions around which it is built—the old versus the new,
imagination versus intellect, black versus white, even country versus
city—are familiar in his work. In terms of quality, however, it is a
failure and to speak of the poor critical reaction as being brought
about by the novel method of punctuation is to miss the point
completely.

The major fault seems to me to be the wretchedly prolix style,
which for a man who prides himself on being a fine storyteller is all
the more inexplicable. One claim that the Baron makes, at least,
would probably win the agreement of the author. When he says,
"...a good yarn is always more satisfying than the truth"[18] he is
merely endorsing what Herbert himself was to say later in the
foreward to his collection of stories *Larger Than Life*. It appears to
be a maxim, though, that he has forgotten in this book. The yarn is
dominated by homily, and an examination of the style shows that
even the homily is couched in a language that seems almost wilfully
meandering. It is marked by a stiffly oldfashioned and ponderous
diction, frequent inversions of the word order for no discernible
reason, and sentences burdened with an almost endless succession
of parenthetical phrases and clauses. Totally absent is the richness
and vitality of the language of *Capricornia*.

One of the most admirable qualities of Herbert as a novelist is his
determination never to repeat himself; hence his burning of the
manuscript of *Yeller Feller*. The price of this ambition, though, has
been that every new work must seek out its own direction, must be
a new way of doing things. *Seven Emus* was a new direction. Its
importance is primarily that it freed the novelist's imagination and
opened the way to proceed to more major tasks.

CHAPTER 4

Soldiers' Women

A gap of twenty-three years appeared between the publication of *Capricornia* and Xavier Herbert's second major novel *Soldier's Women* in 1961, just as a further gap of fourteen years separates that novel from Herbert's third and last ambitious work *Poor Fellow My Country*. In his determination to write something completely different from *Capricornia*, Herbert departed from the territory of most of his previous writings—northern Australia and Queensland—and for the only time in his life dealt with an urban society, a city which is not named in the novel but which is almost certainly Sydney or something very like it. The idea for the novel came to him, Herbert claims, from his observation of Australian women during the war when their men were away. In fact, it probably came earlier than that, as this passage from *Disturbing Element* suggests:

> During that period, eighteen months or so, Mother lived a life that to her must have been about perfect. It was surely the effect of the removal of male domination, and was probably common to women with their dominating menfolk at war. I've heard her sigh in recollection of it years later: "What a wonderful time we 'ad then, just you two boys and I. Remember the sow's ear and the fat week and the lean week?"[1]

Herbert is talking about World War I, of course, but no doubt there is contained here the seeds of *Soldiers' Women*, which is a study of a group of women and their conduct—especially sexual conduct—during World War II. Like Herbert's other two major novels, it is very long (four hundred and ninety pages), densely packed with detail, and deals with enormously ambitious themes.

At one stage Herbert had planned to call it *Of Mars, the Moon, and Destiny*, before returning to its actual, less pretentious title, but the abandoned title gives us a clue to the themes with which the novel deals. Mars is the god of war, symbol of the aggressive instinct that leads men to commit brutalities against one another. The moon is the controller of the tides and also a symbol of woman's sexual impulses, regulator even of her menstrual periods. Destiny is a word which Herbert has always been fond of using, often in a very nebulous context, and in this novel it is invoked constantly in regard to the question of how far men and women are able to control their own "destiny" or how far it is decided for them, without their will or knowledge. All three concepts are major concerns of the novel. It remains to be added, however, that they are dealt with in the novel with very mixed success. Though Herbert's attempt to move wholly outside the territory he knows best and had always previously written about is admirable, *Soldiers' Women* strikes me finally, and reluctantly, as a novel in which the intentions are abundantly clear but the achievement grossly flawed. In particular, there is an obsessive stridency and enormous repetitiveness about the writing that suggests an author not wholly distanced from his material.

One can, as Harry Heseltine does in his booklet on Herbert, write about the novel in almost wholly exegetical terms; but critical integrity compels one to add that, especially compared to the greatness of *Capricornia*, the novel is very much less than an artistic success. Part of the reason for this, at least, is the stubbornly eccentric notions, especially as to female sexuality, that inform the book, as well as the insistence and didacticism with which they are pressed upon us. Part of it too, equally clearly, is Herbert's obvious uneasiness in creating an environment that is so foreign to him, the manifestation of this unease being the too profligate and calculated care with which he attempts to fill out the texture of the novel.

I   *Mars*

Soldiers' Women is set in wartime, even though the actual war itself has almost no part in the action. The symbol of war, and for male aggression in general is the planet Mars. It makes its first appearance very early in the novel when the observant Pudsey remarks "And look at that red star—like God's eye looking angry!" an image the author himself repeats later: "The planet Mars hung in the pearl and amber above silhouette of funereal pines and the stack of the crematorium."[2] At the end of chapter seven Mars is associated with women and love, and this dichotomy is carefully sustained throughout the novel. In chapter twelve, for instance, Herbert repeats his reference to "the crescent moon and ruddy Mars, symbols of Woman and Man, of Love and War"[3] and the suggestion seems to be that it is man's disposition to fight as it is woman's irresistible impulse, especially at certain times of the month, to make love. When Lolly Mulberry and Tudy La Plante ride up to the top story of their hotel Herbert speaks of "a bower furnished in green and gold with gold lace curtains through which peeped the golden moon, the crescent moon, moon of young love but half realized . . . while over the moon's shoulder glared Mars impatient for the testing,"[4] and the two are continually spoken of as being in conflict, or at least competition. In the same passage the "light of the Lamp of Love" is opposed to the "glare of the God of War"[5] and later "the smiling moon and glaring Mars,"[6] and Mars is also described as "the master of all the madness."[7]

In this last phrase may be found a clue as to how Herbert regards the whole phenomenon of war. Since military activity has almost no place in the actual novel (it appears only on the periphery of the action in that Fortitude, beloved son of Materkins La Plante, is killed in action), we have to deduce what Herbert feels about it from incidental remarks. Much of the time he refers to it, in emotionally neutral terms, as a testing ground for "laddies," but fairly late in the novel there is an argument between Rosa and Private Jack Blackstock concerning the morality of war, in which Blackstock makes an impassioned speech about the cynicism of those who promote wars: "What do you know about war? I've been through it. I tell you it's just a big racket—power-getting, bullying, by inferior types. No matter side, they're all the same."[8] Since Blackstock later shows a real love for Rosa and there are strong hints that he and Rosa will retire together to the country, symbol and source of innocence as against urban corruption and promiscuity, it is very probable that these are the author's views as well.

II   *The Moon*

Much more central to the novel, however, is the image of the moon and its connection with female sexuality. As Heseltine points out, the moon is associated quite directly throughout the different phases of the novel with its particular actions. It is alternately a moon of love, when it shines on those of whose amorous activities the author approves (such as Colonel Leon and Serena), and a "moon-witch brooming to the zenith drawing the tides and the adverse destinies of the world behind her"[9] when it shines down on scenes of promiscuity or abortion, both of which are strongly condemned in the novel. As with everything else in the novel, the author's ideas are spelled out specifically, above all in two passages.

The first of these occurs in chapter fourteen where Herbert counterpoints a boring lesson to a classroom of girls on geometry (mensuration) against what is their much more important concern—menstruation:

> *Our subject is menstruation, by which is measured the rhythm of woman's life. Live by that rhythm and you will be happy. The word "menstruation" derives from the Latin mensis, a month, actually the revolution of the Moon. Thus we might say the Moon is the goddess of womanhood . . . or patroness, if you don't like terms that smack of superstition. Not that the subject is easily dissociated from superstition. Folk-lore is full of strange ceremonies concerning it. You find it hinted at in fairy stories. There is the princess who pricks her finger, faints, hides in a trance from the reality of womanhood till awakened to maturity with the coming of love, the Prince Charming. Woman's rhythm of life, her monthly renewal with her patroness the Moon, is the most important thing in her existence. It is her stability in a world made mad for ever by man's wretched alternating between the tension of sex-hunger and the slap-happy folly of indulgence.*[10]

The gratuitousness of the intervention, virtually a direct authorial address to the reader, suggests the urgency of what Herbert has to say, and in fact the passage contains a great many ideas that pervade the whole novel. The notion of fairy tales, for instance, is an important one and is a consistent metaphor throughout the novel itself. In Herbert's scheme, Pudsey is Cinderella, Ida her Fairy Godmother for whom she provides Fairy-food, and she is also described as goldilocks, as is Pudsey herself as well. Fay Fargo is the First Witch, and images of sorcery and demonology abound throughout the novel. Erica becomes a dragon for her heavyhanded chaperoning of Serena when she is with Colonel Leon, Rosa is the black-browed stepsister, at least in Pudsey's eyes, and Materkins is an ogress who carries her stick like a wand.

More importantly, though, in the passage is Herbert's prevailing idea of women's innate sexual drives, which are governed and symbolized by the moon, and their response to men's harshly described lustfulness. Fairly early in the novel Rosa timidly proposes the notion that there are certain times of the month when women are in heat, like animals, and when the prospect of sexual indulgence seems irresistible to them. Ida turns away from the suggestion in distaste and it is not followed up, but very much later Herbert writes a passage in his own persona, addressing the reader directly, in which he appears to confirm his belief in the notion:

Eve, beloved by Adam, has from the begining stood for wantonness in woman. She has been called wanton presumably for having dealt with her man in her own way, which is to say without consulting the Lord, who must have had disclosed plans for the proper conduct of this stooge he had fashioned for the creature he had created in his own image. The Lord overlooked the fact that, since he modelled woman physically on general mammalian lines in order that she should be "fruitful and multiply", she was bound periodically to enter oestrus, the "ripe-time", in which her whole being would be preoccupied with mating with man. Hence the suggestion that Eve was wanton, which means wilfully wicked, is unfair.

What is surely nearer truth is that she was inclined to indiscretion under the influence of the hormonic tide rising within her, perhaps to the waxing of her patroness, the moon. She was not really wilful, merely forgetful of precepts forced on her by those inclined to live by them. In point of fact, concern for the precepts, the moral rules, was really the duty of Adam at such a time, a large part of his service to protect her during this period of her greatest vulnerability.[11]

Since Herbert really appears to believe in this extraordinary suggestion the surprising thing is that he is so harshly and continually critical of the female characters throughout the novel when they submit to the compulsions he has described. At one point in the novel, it is true, he makes the surprising suggestion that Materkins might have been a more human woman had she kicked up her heels a bit, like her daughter Rosa. For the rest, though, sexual indulgence except with one's marital partner (and of course they are all absent anyway) is severely condemned and punished.

Evidence of the effects of Herbert's own celibacy when writing the novel is abundantly present in the novel. Sexual indulgence is almost invariably punished. Before the novel started, Ida, it is subsequently revealed, became pregnant by her first lover and married Ralph only to provide a father for the child; Rosa also has become pregnant after being virtually raped by her husband on her bridal night. During the course of the novel Pudsey becomes pregnant; Felicia loses her virginity by force to an American soldier and dies from a self-imposed abortion; Lolly Mulberry also becomes pregnant by Fortitude La Plante after only one night; Rosa and Pudsey also give themselves abortions; Fay has had an abortion that left her infertile; and both she and Pudsey become prostitutes for a time. In this extraordinarily fecund world, sexual intercourse is indeed met with swift retribution.

In describing the origins of the novel, in the article quoted from earlier, Herbert wrote further:

I couldn't be bothered writing about war. What interested me was how my comrades were affected by being away from home, particularly their feelings about their women, on account of whom they seemed mostly troubled by what they heard of the doings back home in their absence.[12]

But in point of fact, Herbert wrote virtually nothing about what the comrades away from home felt. With the brief exceptions of Fortitude La Plante (who is given two sections near the middle of the novel before dying offstage) and the woodenly pretentious Colonel Leon, who appears briefly near the end as a kind of masculine ideal for the author, the novel focuses solely on women, and especially women's sexual activity when freed from the normal restraints of husband and family; and Herbert's view of them is, for the most part, a highly cynical one. Most of the women in this novel behave, at least in his eyes, as whores. He speaks, in fact, of "the harlot that's in every woman."[13]

III   *The Women*

The bulk of the novel's attention is given to Ida Fry, the surname presumably suggesting her eventual fate, who is portrayed as vain, malicious, cowardly, promiscuous and a woman who lives solely for appearances. Before her marriage she had followed the profession of beauty-culture; the preoccupation with externalities and appearance to the exclusion of everything else pervades her whole life. Her innumerable dresses from Ramona Kelly are described in precise detail. The suggestion that her beauty is a purely manufactured, artificial thing is crudely reinforced by frequent mention of her dental plate—Herbert seems to have the same fascinated revulsion against false teeth Patrick White has—and the whole empty vanity of her life is perfectly epitomized in the account of one day which consists of nothing but dressing carefully, discussing in detail new trends in fashion, and then finally sallying forth to have an already perfect appearance worked on for several hours by the Salon Gerard in Fashion Street, after which she emerges, Herbert tells us, looking much the same as when she went in.

Like Belinda in *The Rape of the Lock*, her dressing is comparable to a religious ceremony and Ramona Kelly's is often described in imagery suggestive of a temple or house of worship. Far from being the Fairy Godmother of Pudsey's imagining, Ida is characterised by Herbert with brutal directness as a whore, which is also how he describes Rosa:

All that had been said was that was no time for a woman to be having babies while men were indulging in their periodic lad-testing with murder called war. Was the freedom wanted for woman's indulgence in the excitement of war, which is some kind of whoring after warriors? It might well be so. For they made a curious combination this pair. One might be said to be a whore by disposition, but lacking the forthrightness that makes a true whore, needing a strong nature to lean on in her wilfulness while yet she might lead that strong one whither she herself inclined. Such a strong nature was the other's, and she was right ready to be led because she lacked direction: being inclined to the matriarch which is the antithesis of whoring, but as yet too immature to accept the strict morality of matriarchy, and rebellious against it because bred in its stringency.[14]

Here, as elsewhere, motherhood and marriage are the sole forms of female sexual conduct acceptable in Herbert's strict canon; and abortion, in particular, is seen as an evil, life denying act, described in terms of witchery and "a coiled thing like an adder with one eye."[15]

There remains one more curious thing about Ida. In addition to the series of male lovers she takes with such avidity in the course of the novel—Bill, Colonel Van Vrink, Jed Jansen, to say nothing of those such as Colonel Leon, Corporal Cody, the British officer Eugene, Detective Tacitus with whom she tries but fails—she appears to hold an irresistible attraction for women also. In her very first appearance in the novel she and Rosa are explicitly described as lovers and it quickly becomes apparent that she attracts many women quite unconsciously in the same way. Herbert finally makes the point in overt terms: "Ida with her dainty frailty and little-girl's selfishness was just the type to attract Lesbian affection. No doubt about it, the attachments of Selina and Erica to her were of this order, innocently so, of course. Likewise would it be and more so with that wizened little capon, Mrs. Pewsey."[16] To which one could certainly add Rosa and Pudsey, and perhaps even Madeline as well.

On Rosa, Herbert is not quite so severe, as the passage quoted above suggests, partly because her marriage (and consequent need of an abortion) is hardly of her own making and partly because, unlike Ida, whose cowardice is constantly symbolized by her refusal to look interlocutors in the eyes and whose callousness on the death of her children almost defies credibility, she is courageous and does have a maternal instinct. She shows much more shame and remorse than Ida after she has taken a lover and at the end, having been punished and learned from her contracting of venereal disease, seems to be headed for a life of reform in the country with Private Blackstock.

The third main character is Pudsey, who receives almost as much attention as Ida and with whose life her own constantly intersects. In the early stages of the novel she is a not unsympathetic character, and at this stage Herbert's feeling towards her are curiously faltering and ambivalent. Even at the end, despite her horrible murder of Fay Fargo, we never quite lose sympathy for her, as being in many ways a victim of forces outside herself.

Early in the novel Pudsey resembles Christina Stead's Louie in *The Man Who Loved Children*. She, too, is talented and imaginative, physically unattractive, cursed with a mother she does not like and who, it is alleged, she has tried to poison; but having ambitions of becoming a writer also. Aged only fourteen years and ten months, plunged into a world of adult vice which she could not possibly be expected to cope with, her corruption is inevitable. Her final, reluctant acceptance of her first lover Athol is shown virtually as something on which she has no choice: "It was Pudsey who gave in, surely because further dealing with this man was her destiny."[17]

Herbert's stance in regard to her moral responsibiltiy is a curious one and difficult to define. Here, and elsewhere, he speaks constantly of her in terms of her fate and destiny, and yet he withholds sympathy throughout most of the novel. Even her final redeeming action, attempting to save Ida's two children from the fire at Shellybeach, is not dwelt upon. It is likely that Herbert rejects the notion of environmental determinism, placing stress instead on what he sees as far stronger biological imperatives. Shortly before her brutal murder Fay Fargo makes an impassioned and quite moving defence of herself, arguing with justification that she had never had an opportunity to live decently:

I've been ill-treated all my life. My father was a mongrel who starved and belted me and my other, till he deserted us when I was only eight. My mother died when I was ten. And when I was twelve my foster-father seduced me, and my foster-mother put the blame on me and threw me out.[18]

Such a catalogue of disasters should surely incline one towards sympathy and there is, besides, a fairly ready fund of vulgar tolerance and good will about Fay, at least until the time she goes back to jail. But this speech of hers is followed by the instruction of the didactic lighthouse, a device Herbert introduces to augment the considerable amount of homiletic wisdom he has already distributed among his readers:

What said the lighthouse now?

Female virtue is not accident. It is inherent in the womb for protection of the species. But it is to be found only in wombs fully female, not in hens that crow or women that whistle. Whores are not made, they're born.[19]

This, it would seem, is a judgment not merely of Fay but of Pudsey as well.

The other female characters are less important. Materkin, Lollita Mulberry, Madeline, Felicia, Pixie and a whole host of subsidiary characters make an appearance and some of them suffer the consequences of their erratic sexual conduct. This is, in fact, a novel concerned almost exclusively with women and apart from Frank Dalby Davidson's *The White Thorntree* (which is such an anachronism that it might better have been named *The White Elephant*) it would be the longest and most obsessive Australian novel ever to attempt to deal seriously with the question of female sexuality.

IV   *Herbert's View of Sexuality*

I have suggested that even in plot terms many of the characters suffer because of sexual indulgence, in the swift retribution with which it is met. However, there are two further ways in which the author makes abundantly clear his opinion of sex outside marriage. One is in the frequent passages of authorial comment with which the book is studded. Herbert has always had a tendency to intervene in his narratives but in *Soldiers' Women* the intrusions are frequent, blatant, and like everything else in the novel, repetitive. As early as the first chapter Herbert describes the weeping of Pixie Batt as "snivelling" and then makes mention of her two children, adding coldly "the babes of her extravagant self-pitying no doubt."[20]

This kind of authorial judgment becomes more common as the novel goes on until eventually, not satisfied with making judgments and giving advice in his own person, Herbert adopts the device of the lighthouse which continually spells out messages which the protagonists ignore at their peril. These reach their crescendo in the final section when Colonel Leon and Selena are contemplating having an affair, and, in the sole example of female renunciation in the novel, Selena decides against doing so. Flashes from the lighthouse are intercut with pieces of sage advice from Leon, perhaps as woodenly and offensively didactic an authorial spokesman as has ever been conceived.

One would not feel the jarring presence of so much homily if it were not of such a clichéd kind. Herbert seems to have come up with almost every sententious aphorism about female conduct he could have thought of. He speaks of "that smirking insolence with which women customarily settle down to a tete a tete";[21] expatiating on love he speculates, "What is love? But love is no true need of man's. It is woman's need. It is man's weakness to meet it, and it is his destiny, part of his fulfilment if the woman's need is honest, his damnation if it is otherwise."[22] Nonsense like this abounds: "Playing indifference is rightful for a woman, but only spiteful for a man";[23] "Possession may be nine points of law: but it is true need to possess that is the true strength of possession";[24] ". . .is it really womanly and not a kind of inverted masculinity that inclines women to seek power through eroticism that is not truly erotic? Does not true eroticism in the female belong to nature, as far beyond control of will as the tide pulled by the moon?";[25] "Eden was lost to humankind not through Eve's perfidy, but through Adam's greed";[26] "a man is not really as old as he feels, but as old as he is made to feel by woman";[27] "Woman, made for suffering, rather than be without suffering will make it for herself";[28] "Despite his polygamous tendencies, the average man's heart belongs to only one woman: mother, sister, first sweetheart, or wife";[29] ". . .what is a man's resolution against a woman's?"[30] On and on it goes. It seems hardly necessary to say that metaphysical speculation has never been Herbert's strong point as a writer—he is far too intuitive for that—but in the latter stages of this novel the writing degenerates into mere sloganeering.

Herbert has spoken of himself (correctly, as far as his best work goes) as not being a moralist, and has shown, in explaining his own writing, a sophisticated grasp of the extent to which aesthetic objectivity and distancing are important in a work of art. In *Soldiers' Women* that distancing is frequently absent; and this manifests itself not only in the didacticism referred to but in the horrified and nauseated tone in which the author describes sexual misconduct (which in this novel equals sexual conduct of almost any kind) and the crudely moralistic tones he uses to describe and rebuke his characters. Only Serena escapes his censure (though he allows some sympathy for Rosa) since, although tempted by her love for Colonel

Leon, she finally renounces him for her husband and children. For the rest, the tone in which Herbert describes the various instances of fornication is filled with horror, revulsion and contempt.

Continually he intervenes in the narrative to direct our moral responses towards the characters. Ida and Pudsey are described as "sinful women"[31] and "sinful ones" when they dance with American soldiers. Fay and Pudsey are "waifs on their inevitable way to Hell"[32] and Fay is constantly referred to as "Theodora the Damned." Pudsey slinks "like the hunted criminal waif the processes of her destiny had made of her"[33] while Ida and Rosa are called "wantons." Even their dressing comes in for criticism; when Ida gives Rosa a more attractive hair style Herbert baldly calls it a "strumpet's hair-do."[34]

More pervasive even than the direct abuse is the tone in which sexual encounters are described. Herbert is concerned to stress the sacramental nature of love but in his anxiety to do this he is led into language which at times falls little short of hysterical abuse. The conception of sexuality and its expression generally is as animalistic, physically gross or even obscene, the product of undiscriminating and avaricious need. Sexual encounters are short, violent, loveless, and followed by the males, at least, behaving like sated pigs. Ida's first experience of infidelity, for instance, is described in terms that would do justice to the worse of novelettes:

Bill looked in leering: then he bored in, guffawing when she squealed and tried to cover up her nakedness. And he tore the cover from her, gasped at the sight of her, stared: then seized her despite her desperate pleas, silenced her with frantic kisses, flung her on the bed amongst her pretty things, and fumbling and snorting and bucking like a berserk beast, dealt with her in the ancient way.[35]

There is much dealing with women "in the ancient way" in the novel, no new way having apparently been devised by its male characters; and both individually and *en masse* the soldiers are merely animals whose activities, even to eating ("the human hogs at their swilling")[36] are described in tones that border on the nauseating. Pudsey's first lover is "a faun with the head of a young lion and the conduct of a billy-goat,"[37] and La Boheme where the party takes place is "a glittering bawdy-house." At the same party Felicia becomes involved with a "laddy as innocent as herself to begin with, though liking his condition not: and he became by midnight so maddened by the unseen rut as to try to drag her to a bower to strive for their mutual debasement to the common level." Later Pudsey is left "at the mercy of Plug, who leapt upon her without delay and dealt with her in the ancient and horrible way of the human male."[38] But the most hysterical language is reserved for Pudsey's initiation into Mary Ann's brothel, an admittedly horrible enough experience in itself no doubt, but described in a tone that is too excited to convey the experience with any clarity or conviction:

So up in a brandy whirl to the bower of fake violets . . . then to be swept into a mirror-walled maelstrom of slobbering mouths and glaring eyes and, monstrosity of all monstrosities, the rampant phallus . . . to be beaten down by wave upon wave of reeking lust . . . to be smothered . . . to be drowned in filth . . . to be outraged till she cried for mercy, for help . . . help, help, help![39]

Possibly this is Pudsey's consciousness being rendered, but one doubts that she would use language like "rampant phallus," and in any case there is no evidence of the author's detachment from the character.

In the rare cases where some pleasure is actually experienced from sexual intercourse, Herbert describes the characters in terms of physical appetites and satiation, again suggesting nothing but animality. And it may be worth remarking at this point that of the many images that Herbert employs repeatedly in the novel, the most ubiquitous as well as the most protean are images of animals and birds.

To take only some of the most common, Pudsey is in turn a hibernating toad, Pat the Batt, a wounded little animal, a wounded cockatoo, a snipe, and a frightened blue-eyed cornered snake. Her voice is variously described as an uncombed cockeral's voice, that deep goat's bleat and that capon's crow, and Herbert also says of her that she screeched "Like a cockatoo."[40] Even her hair is described in a series of equine images.

Ida is called upon to make an even more astonishing series of transmogrifications. She is first of all a fish, then a squeaking mouse, an oriole, a dainty canary, and a masked finch. With Rosa, she is one of two pretty hens (and Rosa, incidentally, is a silly fat rabbit, a weasel, a blue wren in a flock of soot sparrows and a plump brown chicken as well).

The point does not need further emphasis. Suffice it to repeat that Herbert's forte has never been psychological verisimilitude or the conveying of the inner life of the characters. His characterization tends to be very much from the outside, in terms of motifs, consistent patterns of imagery, the creation of an intense and varied universe which is not merely a naturalistic but a metaphorical one. In *Capricornia* this method is highly successful; in *Soldiers' Women*, for some of the reasons I have tried to show as well as others I want to come back to later, it is not. The habit of characterizing human beings in terms of animals was present in *Capricornia* to some extent, grew more common in *Seven Emus*, and by the time we get to *Soldiers' Women* has grown quite out of hand. Even minor characters, some of whom appear only once in the novel like Siggy ("a gold-combed rooster,"[41] "that gilt ape"[42]) are given the treatment; and once an image is introduced Herbert tends to hang onto it for grim life.

Not only does the author apply metaphors drawn from the animal and bird world to the characters in his expository prose but the *characters* do so among each other in their dialogue as well. In their discussion of Athol, for example, the rhyming Americans Ossie and Mossie and Fay Fargo manage in the space of about two pages to call him successively a zebra, horse, skunk, rattle-snake, tiger and bunny-faced bastard. The technique reaches its culmination in the figure of Roddy the Rodent, who is dehumanized to the point where his whole nature and existence are characterized purely in rodential metaphors; he has no anthropomorphic features at all.

This somewhat mechanical, externalized method of characterization betrays itself further in Herbert's continual habit of coupling two characters of opposite types. Diametric pairs appear throughout the novel in mathematically logical arrangements. By far the most important, of course, are the main two women, Ida and Rosa, whose different complexions are constantly pointed out. But of the more peripheral figures there are their first pair of would-be lovers, Sergeant Jansen and Corporal Hooley. Jansen is a bear, "a red bear, with face ruddy-shiny as the rising sun"; Hooley is a wolf, "lean and dark and tall as the slippery-dip . . . and with shiny teeth and the howl of a whole wolf-pack."[43] The second pair they take up with are Captain Brand and Captain Kahn, who are seen as Perseus and Phaeton: "Perseus was dark, Phaeton auburn, brown eyes and blue."[44] The next pair are similarly chosen to set each other off, "a ruddy, fair-haired square-headed bear-man first-named Bill, a lithe brown leopard-man named Dolphin."[45] Two of Miss Blister's stu-

dents are matching flowers, Jonquil and Poppy. The strangers
Pudsey meets at Central Station are described as "a plump motherly
woman, a lean taciturn man."[46] Ossie is the friend of Mossie (there
are also a Hike, Mike and Spike, as well as Ida's rhyming children
Roy and Joy). Ida and Rosa are the symetrical Sun Queen and
Rainbow Queen pair. Spider and Plug are both huge but the two
are "not uniform in hugeness, one's being in breadth rather than
height, the other's the converse."[47] Private Blackstock is "tall, dark,
aquiline, piercing of grey eye, a man of few words and strong
decisions by the look of him"; his companion Corporal Cody is "a
big fair boy, scarcley bearded, with violet eyes that looked both shy
and sly, a full-lipped mouth twitching all the while as if with
something comical to say."[48] In all these ways, then—rhyming pairs,
matching patterns of imagery and metaphor, and the carefully
diametric physical descriptions of the soldiers—the novel bears the
mark of an over-deliberate hand, of a writer who is not instinctually
one with his world as Herbert was in *Capricornia*, but who has to
consciously "work it up."

There remains one further point to make about Herbert's treatment of sexuality in the novel. One conclusion he has clearly drawn
from his observation of women is that they very often feel an
attraction, perhaps again under the influence of the moon, to each
other as well as to men. Lesbianism is not mentioned specifically,
nor does an overt Lesbian make an appearance, until well into the
novel, but as I mentioned earlier in connection with Ida and Rosa it
is present almost from the first page. Lesbianism in particular, and
sexual confusion and interchangeability are major themes of the
novel. Ida and Rosa themselves are described in terms that suggest
quite plainly a lovers' courtship and throughout the novel there is
an intense, if unexplained, sexual attachment between them. They
smother each other in endearments and embrace with the passion of
lovers. Rosa very quickly comes to take on the protective, "male"
role towards the other woman.

But Lesbianism and sexual ambiguity are not limited to these
two. Apart from Ida's series of quasilovers mentioned earlier, several
of the characters are shown as having masculine features. The most
obvious, of course, is Materkins who is constantly compared to a
tiger and who suffers a kind of sexual misplacement which in the
end she quite specifically enunciates: "I, though a woman, have a
man's mind, can think only in a man's way, achieve only as a man
achieves, but, being a woman can achieve only through a man and

a man who must be truly mine, bone of my flesh, flesh of my flesh, a masculine projection of myself, created by myself."[49] Her relationship with her incongruously named son Fortitude is essentially that familiar concern of Herbert's, that of a domineering father towards an inhibited son. Its equivalent in the novel is that of Pudsey, who is spoken of as "one who had always been a daddy's girl anyway,"[50] and her father, except that, like most of the men in the novel, the latter is woefully weak. Tudy is unable to relate to women in an adult way, and although Lolly is finally able to separate him from his mother and send him off to war, she can do so only by taking over her role as quasiparent. Herbert says pointedly of their sexual union that Lolly "seduced him into incest."[51]

Less dramatically, Fay is often spoken of as looking like a boy while even Pudsey is "a quaint little figure like a dumpy boy, only for that over-developed bust."[52] Herbert speaks specifically of Lesbianism in connection with feelings towards Ida in chapters five and seven, in the former associating it with the moon:

> It was midnight when the moon rose from the sea: a moon long past the fullness of her promise, hump-backed hag-moon, a moon for witches' wickedness, like a peak-faced witch herself. She pried through windows uncurtained to her stare. She stared into the boudoir of the mistress of Shellybeach and moved in Lesbian lechery upon the pale pathetic little cheek.[53]

But it is not until the introduction of the "Lesbo"[54] Birdie that the theme becomes explicit. Significantly, it is the epicene Fay whom Birdie first makes love to, but later the author drops us a broad hint that Pudsey's prostitution involves more than one sex, telling us that "Birdie has a weakness and Pudsey knew it and was not above playing up to it: and thus she got much of what she wanted out of her."[55]

V   *Destiny*

Herbert's third central theme is that of Destiny, a word which he uses in various and often contradictory forms throughout the novel. We have noticed Herbert's concern with destiny, or fate as he sometimes calls it, throughout his fiction, but nowhere is it more pervasive than here, where he seems torn between a theory of biological imperatives and one of environmental determinism. At one point in the novel, a representative of the law, the chattering

Miss Birdfinch, talks to Pudsey of God's design on earth. She says, "So you can see God's design in what people mistakenly call an imperfect world. It's our job to make it perfect. That's the meaning of our existence, don't you think?"[56] Since this Rousseauian view is represented through a figure of legal authority, a group whom Herbert rarely treats with sympathy, it is not surprising that the rest of the novel is largely a contradiction of it.

Herbert's own philosophy is enunciated in specific terms by the didactic Colonel Leon late in the novel; in a long speech on anthropology he makes to Selena he says:

> A thousand million years—but mere numerals can't convey a tithe of the meaning of the vastness of that time. A thousand million years: it can be comprehended only in terms of evolution, and then not merely intellectually. . . . Individuals beyond computation there have been. Yet each strove for fulfilment of its own individual destiny, hence strove for the destiny of its species, and ultimately for perfection of the stupendous purpose that is back of it all. . . . The idea of God the Father stood as the first and ever-present reality once upon a time. Replace that with the rational idea of the high destiny of mankind as the be-all-end-all, with the belief that it is a matter of inevitability to strive for Man's perfection, as it was to bow before the Glory of God. Then the great truth of our evolution would surely be before us all the while: we would have one great purpose, and our pettiness should vanish. There would then be two main virtues to acquire and keep: courage and kindness.[57]

These extracts from a very much longer conversation between Colonel Leon and Selena represent the essence of his—and one feels certain, the novel's—philosophy. They show the progress of his thought from a kind of Darwinian theory of evolution, through a rejection of orthodox Christianity and the sunny, platitudinous optimism of Miss Birdfinch, towards an ethic based on the notion of human perfectibility. But just as Leon speaks here of the "inevitability" of this process so does the novel repeatedly insist elsewhere that the characters' *evil* destinies are as inevitable as their virtuous ones. Herbert, in other words, introduces the notion of will, of autonomy over one's fate, merely to cast serious doubt over it. When Pudsey in a moment of generosity offers Ida Jansen's telephone number, knowing that she will have no further use for it, Herbert remains unmoved and sceptical: "Can one's acts be kind that are done against one's will? But how much of what one does for others does one truly will?"[58] He speaks continually, especially in

regard to Pudsey, of "Destiny," implying that it is something
beyond her control and therefore inevitable, which makes his lack
of sympathy for her all the more surprising. Early in the novel,
Pudsey is confident of her own "high destiny"[59] as the author calls
it. It is not long before we come to see that Pudsey is doomed to a
fate very much grimmer than she has imagined.

The foreboding tone is constantly present. In her relationship
with Athol, who initiates her into sex and is probably most responsible, at least after Ida, for her downfall, it is repeated almost
continually. Herbert's pointed disdain for the characters and their
actions manifests itself not merely in an absence of sympathy but in
a positive gloating over their ultimate impotence. As they are about
to separate he says, "It was Pudsey who gave in, surely because
further dealing with this man was her destiny."[60] When again she
tries to leave him and he asks her if she is rejecting him Herbert
comments: "It was a challenge. She struggled for a moment to meet
it. But some need of hers or his beat her."[61] Shortly afterwards he
speaks of "the compulsive journey to her high destiny,"[62] the
adjective clearly intimating the element of willessness or coercion.
Gone now is the confidence and eagerness with which she had
looked forward to life; the phrase "high destiny" is now purely
ironic, as it earlier was not.

If Pudsey is the chief focus of Herbert's beliefs about destiny it is
also true that the theme becomes a major object of his attention in
the last parts of the novel, where the story of Ida and Jansen is
juxtaposed very pointedly against that of Selina and Colonel Leon,
and the authorial judgments there amplify what one of the quota-
tions above only intimates—that one's destiny, the relationships into
which one enters, even the emotions one has towards other people,
are largely the product of need.

Herbert says at one point, again in regard to the relationship
between Athol and Pudsey, "Chance brings people together. The
play of the needs of their individual destinies does the rest. There is
no gainsaying those needs."[63] This is the philosophy of the novel in
a nutshell. The concept of need is associated at different times with
admiration ("True love cannot be offended: for admiration is one
half of it, the other half need; and admiration implied accepted
inequality, hence humility");[64] with attachment (Rosa knew "intuitively that their attachment was based on need one of the other");[65]
with friendship ("What is the basis of friendship? Is it not need?");[66]
and above all, with love ("She had encouraged him to this point.

Whether it would develop into love depended on his capacity to meet her primary needs").[67]

Statements such as the latter are particularly common in the later juxtaposed sections dealing with Ida and Jansen, and Selina and Leon, where Herbert seems to be frantically concerned that he has not made his philosophy sufficiently clear, and where the lighthouse is particularly voluble in its sermonizing. But the effect, sadly, is again to treat human relationships in a demeaning and simplistic way. It is to posit a crude kind of determinism, even admitting that Herbert's definition of "need" would be a very broad one: the kind of need that Ida satisfied in other women, for instance, is not an easy one to explain. And at times, in fact, Herbert virtually admits this determinism: "But is there really any *might* about one's dealings with one's fellows, when the basis of human association is satisfaction of need, and one's need is part of one's destiny, and one's destiny is the expressed meaning of one's existence?"[68]

VI   *Conclusion*

Soldiers' Women is a brave attempt at writing a novel completely different from anything Herbert has written before or since, but much as one admires the author's integrity in refusing to repeat easy triumphs and much as one applauds the ambitiousness of the novel and the skill with which such massive amounts of material are manipulated it seems to me that the unfamiliarity of the whole world of *Soldiers' Women*, by which one means far more than the mere physical locations, finally militates against the novelist's attentions.

The novel is impressively organized and its narrative momentum never flags. Apart from a brief excursion into the point of view of Tudy, involving two sections after which he disappears from the novel for the last time, most of the first two thirds are involved with Ida and Rosa on the one hand, and Pudsey on the other. Then towards the end, the story of Selina and Leon is juxtaposed against that of Ida and Jansen, as offering some kind of ideal of fidelity and self-sacrifice. As always, Herbert is open about his intentions: "Close to the lovers in the boat-shed at Shellybeach that bright and breezy night were the other couple in the romantic parallel, Leon and Selina: close in spatial terms, a mere hundred yards, but far distant in the character of their love."[69] The point is obvious enough anyway, but Herbert's direction of our attention to it spells it out further.

This whole crowded world is organized with considerable skill, and with a scrupulously careful attention to detail. Herbert has worked hard at capturing the texture and feel of the urban wartime society. There are the songs, for instance, which make their way endlessly through the narrative—*In the Mood*, especially, with its obvious relevance to the activities of the characters, *Ain't It a Shame About Mame!*, *Why Do I Love You?*, and all the military songs that the soldiers sing. There is the endless circle of houses, bars, clubs, shops and hotels through which the characters wander aimlessly in their frantic search for pleasure and distraction—Shellybeach, La Boheme, Silvery Waves, Monte Christo, Rosella (where Birdie lives), Azure Court, Montrose; Lobster Bob's, the Jade Chopsticks in Peking Alley; the officers' club Reeba's; the Cairo, the Hotel Harlequin and the Cockaigne Tavern; Ramona Kelly's and the Salon Gerard; the Aloha, Mary Anne's brothel. All are faithfully described, with remorseless attention to detail.

So is what the characters wear. Ida's apparently infinite wardrobe from Ramona Kelly (who seems to supply half Sydney—her dresses even turn up in Mary Ann's brothel) is described in minute detail, from her moss-green Jersette through her maroon slacks and yellow sweater to her white shark-skin bathing suit. Such a mass of superfluous detail surely suggests the strained care with which the author is working to build up his world; there is a selfconscious and inhibited quality about the writing that was totally absent in *Capricornia*.

It is also enormously repetitive and somewhat mechanical. That continual pairing of opposites in which Herbert indulges is only one example of his fondness for patterns of repetition. Many of the establishments seem to be run by "enuchs." Knowing taxi drivers abound. So do fawning waiters and serviles: again Lorenzo at the Genoa, Cholly at the Harlequin ("A little old fellow like a bald-headed hawk"),[70] an anonymous ratfaced lackey, a goat-eyed page, Nicko ("a small black monkey").[71]

Even more distracting are the repetitive tags or shorthand descriptions applied as characterizing gestures: Ida's endlessly mentioned lolly-lip; "straining their potatoes" as a euphemism for urinating; Herbert's listing of the three stages of intoxication; repeated mention of the disapproving eyes of Ida's husband; American voices, described as the "national organ"; the South Head lighthouse; the "telegrins"; the "coiled thing like a one-eyed adder." All these are repeated constantly throughout the novel.

Overlaying the more or less naturalistic pattern of description are more purely metaphorical and figurative patterns. The novel is dense with imagistic allusion; it abounds in motifs and metaphors which, unfortunately, fail to go beyond the function of mere labelling. Mention has been made of the animal and bird images. One could add that many of the characters have the *names* of birds as well— Birdie, Miss Pinkfinch—or of flowers—Jonquil, Carnation, Poppy. Others are compared to flowers. Ida is more than once described as a peony. Rosa, of course, is a rose. Selina is associated with pansies, carnations and frangipanis. Lollita Mulberry is described at one point as a spotted tiger-lily and her mother as a black orchid, copper-tipped.

Many of the patterns of imagery involve the supernatural in various ways—hagiography, superstition, fairy tales, demonology and witchcraft. Pudsey's story, "The Enchanted Cat," is a fairy tale and there are many references to Cinderella and the Fairy God-mother and her black-browed stepsister. as well as to Goldilocks. Mention of devils and harpies occurs frequently, especially during the abortion scenes, hovered over by the "sorceress moon." Pudsey sums up several strands of imagery when she describes her mother as "a blood-sucking monster . . . . a female spider, a female octopus, a harpy, a zombie, a monster!"[72]

On the other side there is mention of angels, of the Red Knight (the tag for Jansen), of St. Anthony and Sir Galahad, and Rosa is described at one point as "a penitent nun, a Magdelene."[73] That house of destiny, as it is frequently referred to, has overtones of Hell, with its iron gates, and its eventual destruction by fire, the "inferno." Herbert sums up much of this vein when he says, "The players were vanished, the witches, demons, angels, fairies, foolish mortals."[74]

For all the abundance and occasional ingenuity of the imagery, it is in the end rather too much of a bad thing. The relentless insistence with which Herbert presses his ideas upon us is finally exhausting more than enlightening. That moralist whom the author had repressed in himself is given free rein in this novel with the resulting didacticism being evidence of the preacher getting the upper hand over the artist. For his third major novel, Herbert would return to a country and a theme that he knew much more intimately and intuitively.

CHAPTER 5

Larger Than Life

HERBERT has written a considerable number of short stories, especially early in his career before *Capricornia* was published and when he was struggling to establish himself and live as a short story writer. As he tells his best friend Arthur Dibley in a letter written in 1936, in one year alone (1933) he wrote and had accepted for publication no fewer than twenty-two short stories.

In later years he has written far fewer, being moved to express himself only when some exceptional circumstance occurs, of the kind he explains in the preface to his only collection to date, *Larger Than Life*. Moreover, the later stories seem to me to be, generally speaking, inferior to the earlier ones, despite the author's gleefully pointing out the fact that the editors to whom he sent his earlier work were unable to distinguish it from his later stories (which, in any case, is very much a double-edged sword as far as the question of the author's development goes). They are, for the most part, more self-indulgent, more didactic, more anecdotal, lacking the firm structure and discipline of his earlier work. No doubt this can be put down partly to the fact that by this time Herbert is an established author for whom the short stories are a mere sideline; they are not the basis of the somewhat precarious living he was eking out at that time by writing to strict deadlines set by the *Australian Journal* and the Sydney *Sun*.

I *The Form of the Short Story*

Herbert has always had very firm ideas as to what a short story should be and he sets them out clearly not only in the preface to his first volume but as early as the letter to Arthur Dibley and to his wife Sadie prior to publication of *Capricornia*. They must have a plot, development, an ending that surprises or neatly wraps up what has gone before; they cannot be mere literary sketches or slices of life. The accepted masters are such writers as O. Henry and Guy de Maupassant. Such stories are almost miniature novels, although Herbert is frequently preoccupied with the question of whether a good novelist can also be a good short story writer, as well as vice versa. He says in one letter, for instance:

Now, from what I have observed, I do not think that novelists usually can write short stories well. I have read volumes of the short stories of Wells and Gallsworthy [sic] and Harris and whats his name—Lawrence—to name only those that flash into my mind, and I must confess that I did not think they could write short stories as well as I can. Their stories are fine literature, grand character studies; but they are not what I call short stories; they are merely sketches. O. Henry and W. W. Jacobs are pre-eminent as short-story writers, but where do they stand as novelists?[1]

Technically speaking, then, the stories are comparatively conventional—not necessarily in any pejorative sense—and this impression one has of their orthodoxy is likely to be confirmed by Herbert's account of some of the ways in which he conceives his plots. He writes in a letter dated October 3:

I have in mind several ideas for short stories, but I don't wish to use them, because they may make small novels. So assist me in getting plots. I want you to buy me some second-hand magazines of good quality and send them as soon as you can. Several times I have been assisted in concieving [sic] plot by reading magazine stories. Unfortunately my style is so uncommon that few stories are any use to me. I cannot plagiarize. I wish I could. Most magazine story-writing is sheer plagiarism, you know . . .

What I find hardest in tale-telling is the conceiving of an idea. The invention of complications is nothing. Seeing that my stories are all very 'clever' in plot, and that, quite unaided, I have turned out scores of them, it cannot be said that I am unable to get ideas for myself. Were I able to write mere sketches as most short-story writers do, I could turn out seven a week. I am unable to put my hand to any tale that contains a plot not worthy of O. Henry or De Maupassant. Now these men did not write *hundreds* of stories, as do popular magazine writers of today. Their worthwhile efforts only number a couple of score. Why? Because the conception of ideas for tales as intricate as they felt bound to write was difficult. I am in like case yet, during 1933 I wrote and had accepted no less than 22 short stories. Thus I conceived plots at the rate of one a fortnight. Of these only five were got by that process if it were possible. I only made the discovery late in the year; I then found that it was hard to find such ideas.[2]

Herbert then goes on to give examples of the difficulty of finding suitable stories, listing his experience of reading a whole year's copies of the magazine *English Argosy* without finding one idea suitable for use in his own work.

This cannibalization of popular magazines is done by many writers and is arguably a legitimate way of finding material. To employ Herbert's own analogy, "I don't think it is any more plagiarism that is the working of a simple tale of fact that one has heard from someone else."[3] But in any case, one cannot help suspecting that Herbert's reliance on the magazine stories is even less than he makes out here. This is not so much for the reason that he himself believes—that his style is too idiosyncratic and individual. The style in most of the stories from *Larger Than Life* would be quite familiar to most Australian writers and readers. The author for the most part adopts the pose of the storyteller, the yarn spinner, genial, relaxed, usually a moral pragmatist, content to observe and record without passing judgments on the doings of the characters, which are very often of a disreputable kind.

To take only the most obvious example, racism is never far from Herbert's imaginative preoccupations (except in *Soldiers' Women*) and *Larger Than Life* is full of documentation of the continual and almost unconscious mistreatment of other races by the whites of the communities of Northern Australia. Occasionally, it is true, he allows himself a pointed intervention. Speaking of the half-caste Rorey in "Rocky the Rig," for instance, he remarks, "Disorderly conduct was their commonest offence, meaning to say more or less violent disputation with people who presumed to be their betters."[4] But more often the point is made implicitly, as in the story "Come On, Murri!" which concerns a black boxer who more or less surrenders a fight because of his affection for his white opponent, only to have his friendship thrown in his face; or in casual remarks, such as the assumption in "Look Into My Eyes!" that because none of the whites will submit to the hypnotist the half-castes can be hauled in with no thought of their possible objection. But for most of the time Herbert is far too interested in observing and registering to preach homilies, and his work is all the more effective for that. His indictment of the conduct of the whites builds up by the sheer weight of the dispassionately recorded evidence.

What is interesting about the stories—at least in retrospect—and what makes them unmistakeably Herbert's own is the material and the whole world in which he was working, and it is worth backtracking a little to see how the concerns and experiences of *Capricornia* can be discerned here in embryonic form. All the stories deal with the same area—Northern Queensland and the Northern Territory —and cumulatively they build a world which has its own assumptions about human conduct, its own geographical boundaries, its own set of characters. It is a world which Herbert is both discovering and creating, and eventually it will become the world of *Capricornia*. The stories of *Larger Than Life*—the early stories at any rate— are not only enjoyable in their own right but important as foreshadowing the later novel.

The opening story, "Sequel to a Song," was one which Herbert originally outlined, in a substantially different form, in a letter from which I have previously quoted, as "Machinations of a Jinx." Like "The Spirit of the Land," this is a phrase which occurs frequently in Herbert's thinking and writing—it is a heading of one of the chapters of *Capricornia*, for instance—and the preoccupation with chance, fate, destiny, to list only some of the names he gives it, is a continual one throughout his work. The succession of natural disasters that pursues the Leesings occurs again in *Capricornia*, while biblical notions of the run of bad luck also appear at the end of *Seven Emus*. Herbert's sense of the potential anarchism of nature is merely one manifestation of his highly ambivalent impulses about the extent to which the contingent is an element in man's life. How important is luck? How far can one detect an order in the universe? How meaningful is the concept of destiny? "Was it luck, or what Lofty Griffin, his mate, called Destiny?"[5] he asks in "Rise and Fall of Jeremiah Stacey;" and questions which are only lightly adumbrated here are examined more fully in *Capricornia*.

More specifically, though, certain references in the stories are repeated in identical or almost identical form in *Capricornia*, as well as in the other novels. The figure of the henpecked husband in "Keeping the Peace" or the Boss in "Look Into My Eyes!" is a frequent one in Herbert's writing and emerges in *Capricornia* with The Shouter, a man of massive authority everywhere—except before his wife. In the same story the name of the wife deserter is Wigmore—that of the repressive magistrate in *Seven Emus*.

As he does in *Soldiers' Women*, Herbert sometimes adopts the device of depicting human beings in his stories in terms of animals. Wigmore, for instance, is "the sad old dog," while later his "dog's face"[6] is spoken of. Roy Kingaroy, the benevolent squatter (rare in Herbert's work) in "Rocky the Rig," is a very similar figure to

Pomeroy in *Seven Emus*. The habit of expressing catastrophe in phonetic form ("Crash!") is one Herbert picked up early and retained throughout his writing career. There is frequent mention of a fact Herbert also makes much of in *Seven Emus*—that an infallible sign of deep emotion in an Aboriginal is the jerking or quivering of his face. There is mention of Copper Creek in "Marrying Money" and "Once a Policeman" and even of the Capricornia Hotel in the former. Some comically appropriate names from *Capricornia* appear in these stories: the policemen Sergeant Bullman and Trooper Kintrap in "Once a Policeman . . ." Tim O'Connor in "Moonshine" strongly resembles the later Tim O'Cannon of *Capricornia*. "Once a Policeman . . ." has a child called Marigold. And so the points of similarity, large and small, proliferate. Whether consciously or not, Herbert was preparing himself in these stories for the novels he was later to write. The characters he writes about—policemen, gangers, men of several races or combinations of races, prospectors, con men—are the same types who later appear in his larger works.

II *Destiny and Duplicity*

Generally speaking, Herbert appears in these stories in the role of yarn spinner. Very often, the stories begin with a phrase such as "at the time this tale begins," "as my story about this fat fellow will reveal" or "The setting of this tale . . . ," clearly indicating that the author sees his role as that of entertainer whose job is to amuse and divert, nothing more serious. This is true, at least, of the earlier stories. At the same time, though, there is a certain thematic continuity running through most of the stories. They are the product of an identifiable vision of life. Two themes, in particular, pervade most of them. One of these, the preoccupation with the nature and function of destiny in people's lives, I have mentioned already. The other, closely related element most of the stories share is that of some form of deception or duplicity. A large number of them are concerned with tricks or deceptions that the characters play upon one another.

Many of the stories end with an ironic twist, a habit Herbert picked up in part from O. Henry, no doubt, but which is also completely consonant with his own philosophy of life. Sometimes the twist is the fault of the human beings involved, sometimes that of Herbert's ubiquitous "fate," but in either case the view of life offered is one of anomaly and frustration. In "Mercy Flight" the irony is that of fate at the expense of the human protagonist: the pilot flukes a landing at his destination on a flight on which he should never have taken off, only to find the object of the padre's benevolence recovered and fiercely contemptuous of his offers of spiritual assistance. In "Rocky the Rig" the duplicity is human and benevolent: the squatter Kingaroy throws a race in order to give the Rorey scallywags something to live for and make them law abiding citizens. In "The Best Laid Plans" the irony, again cosmic, is, in fact, what limits the effectiveness of the story: the robbers execute their scheme perfectly only to come undone when a crocodile capsizes the raft on which they have placed the stolen safe. But the ending is so fortuitous and has so little to do with the logic of the events preceding it that the chiding tone of the title seems a little glib.

"Rise and Fall of Jeremiah Stacey," similarly a story in which Herbert is at his more supercilious, concerns the attempt of a prospector to cheat on an old mate. "Michaelos Is a Miser!," "Miss Tanaka," and "Marrying Money" are all stories about successful deceptions involving marital prospects, while "Look Into My Eyes!," probably the best and certainly the funniest story in the volume, involves a deception by the foreman upon his mates until he, in turn, is outwitted by the boss's mother-in-law. Finally, "Moonshine" is to do with that oldest of all Australian themes, the outwitting of the officers of the law by a likeable rogue living just outside it.

Clearly, the country of *Larger Than Life* is no place for slow-witted citizens. Deceptions pile upon one another. In "Marrying Money," for instance, three suitors approach the newly widowed, rich and therefore eligible Katie Blaize, who owns the Capricornia Hotel in Copper Creek. At first the smooth Englishman Harold Hopewell gains a front running position until he is outsmarted by the Australian prospector Ben—who, in turn, is defeated by the patient district trooper, "handsome Dan Cahoun"—whose motives are carefully left ambiguous. At bottom, the idea is not dissimilar to that of "Rise and Fall of Jeremiah Stacey"—the prospector who believes, falsely, that he has found a claim and selfishly tries to keep it to himself. What is striking about the story, however, is the genial cynicism with which Herbert views the successive attempts of the protagonists to outwit each other.

The view of morality in *Larger Than Life*, then, is not an elevated one. Policemen (Kintrap, the young constable in "Keeping the

Peace'') are over-zealous. Wives nag. Merchants are forever in debt and scheming to get out of it by semihonest means (Saichi Tanaka). Prospectors cheat. All this is observed, however, with what amounts to a benign tolerance. Only in "Rise and Fall of Jeremiah Stacey" is the author openly disapproving of Jerry's attempt to cheat his mate (he calls him baldly "a thief, a cheat," and speaks of his "greed"),[7] and even there the condemnation is softened by his continually showing us Jerry's shame and eventual remorse. For the rest, it is noteworthy that two stories end on a note of unrestrained laughter and the view of roguery generally is that expressed by the wily old Greek Michaelos: "If Thanasis knows [about the trick he has just perpetrated] I'll bet he's chuckling in the spirit, because he did like a swift one."[8]

The pervasive geniality of tone is also contributed to by the fact that most of the stories end happily, often fortuitously so, and often our sympathies are directed towards the trickster or the rogue, rather than his victim. The run of bad luck the Leesings have been having finally ends, though Herbert leaves open the question of whether they have, in fact, been "sung" or not. Ben finally leaves Nat Ah Matt, the "A.T.C. Barragoola," and heads off in a different direction. The mercy flight is completed successfully, if somewhat miraculously. "Rocky the Rig" wins, if only by the subterfuge of the squatter Kingaroy, the fat boy finally overcomes his fears, and the eagle Ned Kelly destroys his predators—and there is no doubt in that story whose side Herbert is on. All three stories concerning attempts to arrange marriages end with a certain measure of justice having been meted out. Tim O'Connor is successful in outwitting the police in "Moonshine" but then retires from his life of crime, and the ending of this story suggests that Herbert may well be working with an eye firmly on the commercial requirements of the format in which he is writing; the proprieties and conventions such as "Crime Does Not Pay" must be observed faithfully. However, if so he does not appear to be struggling unduly under the yoke.

In "The Best Laid Plans," where the criminals come undone, the author is careful not to give them very much individuality; they remain more or less anonymous, ruthless figures with whom the reader is not asked to identify. Perhaps the only really pessimistic story, at least among the earlier group, is "Come on, Murri!" which is one of the few attempts in this collection to confront directly the question of black-white relationships. Marty McGann is a young half-caste with a talent for boxing. Gordon Carey is a good-looking white with whom he becomes such good friends that when they fight in the ring Marty has no heart for it, and virtually wills himself to lose. Having earned the contempt and anger of his own people, Marty then finding that Gordon has no time for him, now that he is champion, in a rage takes him on again bare-handed and kills him. The story ends on an unrelievedly pessimistic note, with Marty on his way to jail, presumably to be tried for manslaughter. It is one of the most sensitive and gloomy stories in the book, and one in which Herbert's pose of raconteur is notably absent.

The problem of the half-caste, the fringe dweller, is, of course, one that recurs constantly in Herbert's work; half-castes appear frequently in this collection. There are also a wide variety of races represented; the North of Australia seems to be something of a pot-pourri of different nationalities even if there is little evidence in this collection that this has led to racial tolerance. Chinese, Japanese and Greeks are represented; there are native Australians of varying degrees. The con man Harold Hopewell is an Englishman, while the police and troopers in the stories generally have Irish names. Herbert also, in "Sequel to a Song," uses that curious, self-invented term "Euraustralian" to describe the half-caste bride of the Chinese Lee Sing.

For all the author's own freedom from racism and vigorous defence of the blacks in Northern Australia he seems a firm believer in national stereotypes, or at least genuine national traits. In "Sequel to a Song," for instance, he comments on the part-Chinese Leesing family that while they "accepted the idea that they were being harried by malevolent forces, the fact had not caused them to abandon all endeavour, as for a certainty it would have had they been more aboriginal of heritage. They were too much Chinese not to keep on striving in adversity."[9] In only the second paragraph of the story (and the collection) he remarks:

Not that the Leesings were unduly proud in their measure of whiteness. Indeed, they were the simplest and most easy-going of folk. They were not simply a mixture of black and white, but had a strong dash of Chinese. People of such breed are usually of much happier disposition than most mixed-bloods, perhaps because they inherit some element from the Chinese side which tends towards complacence.[10]

The notions that certain races have uniform characteristics, and that half-castes, generally, have a difficult time, persist throughout the book. Herbert says of Nat Ah Matt in "A.T.C. Barragoola," for instance, that "Probably his complex of inferiority stemmed from his being of mongrel breed."[11] The Greeks are shown as being exceptionally wily and cunning; the Japanese as being concerned with convention and form, unless, like Sakomoto, they become determinedly westernized. We will meet these stereotypes again in *Poor Fellow My Country.*

III *Development in the Stories*

As I mentioned earlier, Herbert boasts in the preface to his collection of the fact that editors were unable to distinguish his earlier work from his later. The collection itself follows no discernible pattern, certainly no chronological one. Eight of the twenty stories we know were written before *Capricornia*, since the author acknowledges the *Australian Journal* and the *Sunday Sun* for their original publication. In addition, "Kaijek the Songman" he admits in the preface to have been written quite some time ago (1945) and "Sequel to a Song" is almost certainly from the earlier period, since its original conception is in the letter Herbert wrote around 1936, from which I quoted earlier.

It is significant that half of the remaining ten stories in this collection concern themselves, either wholly or in part, with the passion Herbert developed during the nineteen fifties for flying. One suspects that most, if not all these stories, came much later in his career. Two of them at least, "Mercy Flight" and "The Flying Fat Boy," have hardly even the appearance of a consciously composed story (whether based closely on fact or not) but rather of a personal anecdote. The later story even gives way to the fat boy's own narrative in his own words, after a couple of tedious pages of preliminary explanation by the author. It is one of the weakest stories in the book, ending with Herbert's pat psychological explanation, obvious enough but spelled out at length for the undiscerning: "Of course the cause of his over-eating was simply lack of confidence. Stuffing himself with food checked that awful empty feeling of insecurity."[12] It is a disappointment after the gripping description of the near crash itself.

"Mercy Flight," too, has the look of a real life story about it, and contains some excellent descriptions of flying, but again, I found it disappointing. The opening is didactic, which is the anecdotist's privilege perhaps, but the moral question which the story seems to promise to deal with—"Does this cover a flight undertaken to save a soul?''—is quickly dropped, and throughout the story the padre remains so obdurately stupid that the tension between him and the pilot can never be fully developed. There is a revealing touch of Herbert himself in his terse remark about the clergyman "stealing my will to serve a faith in which he could sit there calmly waiting for violent death."[13]

The other three stories about flying are rather better. "A.T.C. Baragoola" is a nicely low-keyed story about a half-caste who becomes an inadvertent hero when he rescues two flyers who had crashlanded, and then becomes the self-appointed air traffic controller at an unofficial air strip. He is happy, basking in the company of the romantic breed of flyers, until joined by another prospector, who proceeds to take over and steal the limelight. The story is marked by the typical Herbert pattern of misunderstanding, though this time not observed aloofly but from the viewpoint of the character Nat Ah Matt, with old Ben fondly imagining that he is affording Nat pleasure by keeping him company, and remaining absolutely impervious to the man's increasingly desperate hints.

"An Eagle Called Ned Kelly," definitely one of Herbert's later stories, contains the author's most explicit statement of his romantic view of flying, as well as his fiercely egalitarian contempt for the "squattocracy," the wealthy graziers, especially those who take to the air. In a long, hortatory, but highly revealing passage, he argues:

Flying, to the natural airman, like sailoring to the true-born seaman, is a vocation. But to the squatter it is simply one of the accomplishments appropriate to his social status, a "done thing," like racing a thoroughbred horse. Just as the horse was in the past an essential part of his knightly sports, his racing, polo-playing, hunting, nowadays it is that mount of all mounts for a man, the aeroplane . . .

The eagle is the airman's symbol of that mystery he calls "the three-dimensional freedom of the air." By this token, could a true-born aeronaut take joy in the destruction of an eagle? If the answer is no, it goes to show how far from being truly of the vocation were the flying squatters of McClintockville, when they had reduced the number of wedge-tails habitually frequenting the district from some half-score to this single bird they were now hell-bent on eliminating.[14]

The story concerns an eagle, named after Australia's most famous outlaw and folk hero, who defeats his armed pursuers by leading them into a willy-willy (or whirlwind) and destroying one of the aircraft that was bent on his destruction.

"Femme Fatale" is not really a flying story but combines the old Herbert habit of the surprise ending with his knowledge of flying and the effects of altitude. A man has been murdered and a black man, Bateman, is accused of the crime. As the sergeant returns home in the aerial ambulance with the body of the victim and with the two men concerned, a hand begins to come out from under the blanket covering the corpse, as if it has come alive. In the resulting reactions of the two men, the sergeant is able to discern that it is not Bateman who is guilty but the white man who attempted to frame him, to keep him away from his daughter, before telling the two men that the hand is swelling merely because of the altitude. It is a clever and effective, if somewhat gimmicky story.

In general, the later stories tend to work less well than the earlier, partly because of the kind of element we saw marring "An Eagle Called Ned Kelly." Herbert is more garrulous and self-indulgent, more inclined to give vent to his rather crusty prejudices. The qualities of stories such as "Look Into My Eyes!," "Rocky the Rig," "Michaelos is a Miser" and "Marrying Money," to name only some of the best, are limited but genuine. They have pace, are often nicely constructed, offer a world richly textured and full of variety, and above all are very funny. Some of Herbert's finest sense of comedy comes out of his observation of incongruities in human beings' reactions to situations of extreme stress.

Very often, these observations tend to debunk the character. In "Rise and Fall of Jeremiah Stacey," for instance, the two old prospectors Jerry and Lofty have quarrelled, and Lofty departs from the camp, leaving behind a reproachful note for his expartner. Herbert notes: "As Jerry read, his remorse subsided. He snorted at the missive, screwed it up, and hurled it at Lofty's favourite goat, which gobbled it."[15] The dramatic nature of the gesture is instantly destroyed.

There is a lovely touch in "Miss Tanaka," when two rich and eligible suitors arrive to court what they believe is the beautiful, elegant and inaccessible Japanese maiden Kitso—who is lying on the bed reading Sexton Blake novelettes. In "Marrying Money" the outraged publican's widow is listening outside the door to one of her suitors wriggling out of his promise to marry her because he believes he has found wealth independently. Herbert writes, "Mrs Blaize at the door was trembling so much that Dan Cahoun had to hold her, and breathing so deeply that he had to clasp her mouth. That it was not mere weakness that caused her condition was evident in the fact that she bit him."[16] Although these examples are relatively lightweight, one can see in them the beginnings of the much richer and more complex mingling of comedy with tragedy that characterizes the mode of *Capricornia*.

IV   *Anarchism in the Stories*

Harry Heseltine has recorded discerningly his surprise that Herbert should end the collection with the story "Last Toss," in which a prospector (again Lofty, aged now sixty-seven: the Lofty of "Jeremiah Stacey" was a year away from receiving his old age pension—at perhaps sixty-four) is at the point of death, and discovers firstly the water that will save him, and then, glittering through its crystal clearness, the yellow gleams of gold that represent the strike he had dreamed of all his life but had finally given up on. Herbert himself had spoken highly of the previous story "Kaejek the Songman," giving it the kind of psychological interpretation to which he is very prone. It is not exactly, though, the notion of "a fatality shaping the affairs of men and nature which is one of the guiding motifs in Herbert's whole canon,"[17] as Heseltine suggests, but something closest to its opposite.

Larger Than Life, and to an even greater extent, *Capricornia*, are filled with an implicit anarchism. Good luck comes as readily and inexplicably as bad and men's control over either is very limited. In "Sequel to a Song" Herbert carefully leaves open the question of whether the Leesing family has been "sung" by old Pandaark, or if so, of what kind of power Pandaark possesses, and what it represents. Possibly he was unaware of the implications of his story, or unwilling to pursue them just then, given the limitations of the genre, and the audience for whom he was writing. But "Mercy Flight," at least, more specifically and totally rejects the padre's view of an ordered universe. The plane lands safely, first because they happened to be lucky, and secondly, because while the padre sat there, praying in his oblivious faith and happiness, the pilot was straining every nerve and limb he possessed to get them both down safely.

CHAPTER 6

Poor Fellow My Country

*P*OOR *Fellow My Country*, on which Herbert worked for ten years, is his latest and, according to the author, almost certainly last novel. It is a massive achievement—eight hundred and fifty thousand words (about a third longer than *War and Peace*), in fourteen hundred and sixty-three pages, and selling at a recommended price of twenty Australian dollars when it first appeared. (It has been said that on publication and after a shrewd campaign by its publishers William Collins, the entire edition of fourteen thousand copies sold out in two weeks.)

I *Herbert's Final Statement*

The novel is an attempt to sum up and crystallize all of the concerns—which by now have become obsessions—apparent in Herbert's earlier work. Thus, once again one of the central characters, Prindy, is a boy with both white and Aboriginal blood in him and he, like Norman in *Capricornia*, goes through several transformations of name. As Herbert remarks, he is "known variously as Prindy, Prendy, Al Roy, Alroy, and such secret names as his black godfathers had conferred on him for use if and when he reached a degree of maturity and trustworthiness."[1] Unlike Norman, however, he never doubts his Aboriginal origins and with an almost supernatural prescience in one so young picks out his own destiny immediately: "Learn me kill him Whiteman die / Dat my Road, my proper road / My Rown Road."[2]

Prindy—eight years old when the novel opens and fourteen when he dies near the end—is one kind of idealized Australian. The other is the white man Jeremy Delacy, fifty-three years old as the novel opens and, in the words of one of his many female admirers, "the last Australian": independent; intensely patriotic and contemptuous of other races (especially those crossbred) except the Aboriginal and Jewish; deeply suspicious of intellectuals and especially academics;

109

and a firm believer in practical and pragmatic knowledge, the kind one acquires oneself directly.

It is on these two characters particularly that this vast compendium of a novel is centered, although such is its scope that the list of principal characters at the front of the book (curiously, Herbert returns to this device after denouncing P. R. Stephensen's use of it in *Capricornia*) numbers about seventy-five and there are almost innumerable lesser personages throughout the book not included there. Herbert ranges over a similarly vast number of concerns and issues that have preoccupied him throughout his life's work.

Central to the novel, of course, is the old issue of racism and nationalism. Herbert is as full of anger at white Australians' despicable treatment of its blacks as ever and loses no opportunity of remarking on the continual inequalities and gross injustices that pervade the whole territory of the novel. The hybrid and mongrelized "culture" of the white Australians is continually contrasted with the true, ancient culture of the Aborigines, of which Herbert reveals a quite astonishing knowledge. There is the same love of the land as in *Capricornia*, of Australia Felix and what the blacks call "Good Fellow My Country," and the same insistence that if he lives in harmony with it man will find the land fruitful and beneficent. There is the familiar motif of treks and journeys, with the white authorities constantly forcing the blacks into flights that often end in disaster; and towards the end even Jeremy is dispossessed of his land by the exigencies of World War II. In addition, there is one new element in Herbert's sense of nationalism in his admiration for the Jewish race, as personified in the idealistic portrait of the Jewish refugee Rifkah, with whom the Aboriginals in the novel instinctively identify.

Not only in its larger themes but also in specific details the book gathers up and repeats elements from the earlier novels. For instance, there is the same contempt for academics and especially anthropologists as despoilers of Aboriginal culture for personal advancement that we saw in *Seven Emus*: ". . . what's the biggest and easiest racket to work as an academic? Why, anthrop!" says Fergus Ferris,[3] and in the person of Dr. Fabian Cootes Herbert shows it at work.

There is the same hatred as in *Soldiers' Women* for anyone who takes up a position of service or servility of any kind whatsoever, even soldiers; people who do this are invariably described as lackeys, servants, flunkeys, or minions. There is the same theory of the three stages of drunkenness as in that novel (repeated in this on p. 288), the frequent invocation of the moon, especially during moments of sexual love, the same detestation of homosexuality as personified in the figures of Fay McFee and Denzil Dickey, the same cockatoo screech that we heard so often in *Soldiers' Women*. There is a further reference to Herbert's familiar disturbers of the peace, the human race, to the whites' infamous murder of the Aborigines by poisoning their flour with arsenic, to the satiric characterization of the "Masters of Mankind," to the view of love being based primarily or even solely on need that we saw in *Soldiers' Women* also; and finally there is even the partial though not complete use of characterizing names, as in Judge Bickering, Constable Stunke and Fay McFee.

Essentially, though, the novel is as its title suggests a study of *Terra Australis del Espiritu Santo—South Land of the Holy Spirit*,. its shabby beginnings as far as the whites are concerned, the dream of Australia Felix, the True Commonwealth with which the novel deals, and what is taken by Herbert to be a crucial period in Australia's history, from 1936 to 1943. It argues the failure of that test, as symbolized in Australians' almost universal flight from what they believed to be an imminent Japanese invasion of Darwin and the fact that, as the dismal epilogue records, very little, if anything, has changed many years later.

II   *The Structure of the Novel*

The novel is divided into three massive sections. The first, *Terra Australis*, is unsubtly subtitled "Blackman's Idyll Despoiled by White Bullies, Thieves, and Hypocrites" and deals with the events of just over a year, from September 1939 when the Beatrice River Race meeting is held to the same meeting the following year.

Book One is dominated, on Jeremy's side, by the attempts of first Lydia (1936) and then Alfie (1937) to make love to him and to enlist him in their patriotic and semifascist schemes. The "Blackman's Idyll" of which the heading speaks presumably refers to the black way of life depicted in the excursions of Prindy and George, once they are able to escape from the whites. The two violent incidents that dominate the section are the disruptions of black rituals leading to the death in the first case of Willy Ah Loy and in the second of Queeny, Nell and George. Both are caused, in varying degrees of directness, by whites meddling in Aboriginal ways. Clancy Delacy, Jeremy's son, insists on Willy disrupting the ceremony of Prindy's initiation in the first case while the second situation is set in train by the white threat to separate Prindy from his mother, and is then continued by the Jesus fixated Queeny.

If the first section shows the idyllic life of the blacks in the actual process of destruction by the whites (although, as I want to show later, their life seems to me to be something short of idyllic in ways that the author does not seem able to acknowledge) the second poses some kind of alternative. *Australia Felix*, or "White man's Ideal Sold Out by Rogues and Fools," covers the period from mid-November 1937, roughly six weeks after the closing of Book One, to September 1939 and the postponement of the races that year, and deals mostly with Jeremy's attempts to discard what people have continually criticized as his "Negativism" and become politically active. He goes South and tries to make over the Free Australia Movement into one which will be intensely nationalistic, freed of its antisemitism and allegiances with foreign dictators, and prepared to acknowledge its obligations in respect to the Aboriginals, whose land white Australians had stolen. The attempts end in ignominious failure and at the end of Book Two Jeremy returns to the North, firmly resolved not to enter into political disputes in the future but merely to live as close to the land as possible and do what he can for the Aboriginals in his own way.

Book Three, the shortest of the three sections, commences in September 1939 and is subtitled "Day of Shame," the title of one of Herbert's short stories also giving an account of the day Australians fled their territory after Japanese bombing raids. It carries the detailed account of events through until some time in the second half of 1942 (throughout most of the novel Herbert is meticulous in documenting time) and then there is a concluding chapter which briefly recounts subsequent events up until some time presumably close to the present.

III   *The Failure of the Novel*

Poor Fellow My Country is a novel of remarkable ambition, written out of a very deep sense of pain and outrage at the failures and abuses of the author's fellow countrymen. The intensity and sincerity of feeling are so apparent on almost every page that it is difficult at times to know what one is responding to—the author's personal agony or the work of art into which he has attempted to transform it. It displays an encyclopaedic knowledge and understanding of Aboriginal customs (in fact Herbert has placed a helpful, though incomplete, glossary of terms at the back of the book). Herbert also has the ability to render a very wide range of dialects and accents, though it must be admitted with varying degrees of success. In the case of the heroine Rifkah, for instance, Herbert speaks of "that engaging accent"[4] but in fact it is something of an ordeal to read. At time she sounds like a foreign heavy out of some comic book, and just as the "East European" Monsigneur Maryzic's speech is marked by the frequent appendage of k's, so that of Rifkah is studded with a profusion of z's and occasional v's at the start of her words: ". . . who wos zis Clancy I find so many people of zis country vont to name zere children for?"[5] or ". . . so beautiful, it mek me, for first time in my life, vont loff."[6]

There is the same impressive marshalling and ordering of vast amounts of material that was noted in the earlier two long novels. There are some very fine, lyrical passages when the author is describing nature and a few particularly memorable individual images, such as the windmill turning on a still day ("A flock of birds, wheeling around it, settling on its sails, only to be started into flight again by gravitation"),[7] or that of the military march in Sydney ("Then the gleaming forest of bayonets, a suspended flickering forest of flame").[8] There are also rare comic moments, especially when Bickering is present, though mostly the comic vitality of *Capricornia* has disappeared under the weight of the author's spleen.

Having said this, however, it is equally imperative to say that the novel is very far from being the masterpiece one hoped it might have been. It is a deeply and pervasively flawed work in ways that ultimately limit its achievement very severely. In particular, Herbert's desperate anxiety to convey his views of what has happened to Australia over the past fifty years and the closeness of his identification with a main character, many of whose limitations and bigotries the reader cannot respond to, have led to the same faltering of his aesthetic powers I pointed to in *Soldiers' Women*.

IV *Jeremy Delacy*

There are several more or less unequivocally idealized characters in his novel—one thinks, for instance, of Rifkah, Nanago, even Prindy—but probably any discussion of it has to commence with the nature and function of Jeremy Delacy, and with his relationship to the author. The others, especially Prindy and Nan, are seen mostly from the outside, perhaps inevitably, given the scheme of the book. Although there are ambiguous indications, especially late in the novel, that the author is mildly critical of some of Jeremy's actions and even personal traits, nevertheless he is clearly very close to being the author's spokesman in both his individual opinions and preferences—of which he has many which he is quick to express— and his examples and his ideals of conduct. He seems a kind of repository of the qualities that Herbert would wish in the ideal Australian-born white man, and his list of accomplishments is impressive. For these reasons it is worthwhile analyzing closely just what sort of man Jeremy is.

For a start he is a veterinarian, as well as more or less self-taught chemist and doctor (he heals himself in hospital, following methods the official doctors advise against). He is an expert horse trainer and breeder and an amateur anthropologist of considerable knowledge. He makes his own excellent beer, which visitors compare to the best European beers, mixes his "famous" cocktails, remarked on again with enthusiasm, and also has concocted an ointment that heals saddle sores with remarkable efficacy. He is extremely attractive to women and immediately has most of the women with whom he has very much to do—Nan, Alfie, Lydia, Bridie, Rifkah—in love with him, to the point where they pursue him eagerly in the face of his discouragement of them; and he is also singularly potent: the only women in the novel with whom he has sexual relations apart from his sterile wife Nan, immediately conceive. He is also an extremely good fighter in one on one situations and it takes four men to defeat him. The only area of activity in the novel in which he fails is weather forecasting.

However, it is not merely his accomplishments that suggest Herbert's identification with him but a whole habit of mind and a constant repetition of opinions which, despite occasional mild criticisms or qualifications of Jeremy, seem indisputably the author's own. Jeremy's view on nationalism, the overwhelming preoccupation of the novel, are surely very much akin to, if not identical with, those of Herbert himself. As I mentioned, Herbert is sometimes overtly critical of his main character;—for instance, he hints towards the end that he was rather too dogmatic earlier and that his city experiences have mellowed him, there is an unexplained rift with Rifkah who seems to disapprove of his political activities, and in a rare moment towards the end Herbert specifically mentions "the smugness of his own self-sufficiency."[9] Nevertheless, the abiding impression we are asked to take away of Jeremy is the one offered by Fergus Ferris, one of many characters in the novel who fawn on him: "You're a perfectionist, Jeremy . . . in an imperfect world."[10]

The question of the nature of Jeremy and his function in the novel is a crucial one because very frequently events are presented in such a way that it is difficult for the reader to know how he is being asked to respond to them—not because of their intrinsic ambiguity or complexity but because no clearly defined authorial stance is perceptible. For instance, what are we to make of the horrifyingly brutal treatment of Savitra at the end of the novel when she stumbles upon the secret initiation ceremony of her betrothed Prindy? As far as one can gather, it is looked upon more or less with equanimity by the author. Why does Rifkah turn upon Jeremy at one stage in the novel? Does the author feel it was justified, that Jeremy has in some way broken his trust? And what are we to make of General Esk, that imperialistic blimp who nevertheless is shown in his dealings with Jeremy in a way that is surely meant to be taken as sympathetic, with the two of them acting like a pair of lovesick schoolkids out on their first date? And where and how does Rifkah fall in love with the improbable Father Glascock (another characterizing name, meant to suggest the fragility of the lovers' sexual relationship)?

As in *Capricornia* Herbert adopts an aloof, omniscient point of view—at least in one sense. It is not the individual personality, the complexities of characterization that absorb him as a novelist, but the overriding pattern the collective blundering of those personalities produces; his ironies are, as usual, cosmic.

Frequently, too, he will demonstrate his aloofness from the narrative in a quite ostentatious way by crosscutting from one scene to another and back again: look, for instance, at the scene of the pursuit of Prindy and George by Nell and Queeny in chapter eight. On one page alone we have three "shots," as Herbert cuts from the man and boy to the women and their dog, back to the men, and then back to the women again. His detachment is noticeably in evidence as he observes: "If only they had followed their own noses then they would have spared themselves a lot of labour and time and perhaps even a great deal more; unless, in the strange circumstances Chance could be utterly ruled out,"[11] with the author playing with the idea of chance but refusing to commit himself. Or again a moment later pointedly dissociating himself from the women's efforts to remain hidden as he comments of the dog Mungus, "He whimpered with impatience as Nell dragged on the

leash to prevent his rushing madly to the top and betraying them.
As if the cockatoos had not done that already to anyone on top."
This detachment tends to be greatest at moments when the blun-
dering of the characters leads to tragic results, as here.

The omniscient point of view is apparent too in the fact that
Herbert often describes events none of the characters in the novel
could have been privy to, or, as in the above case, only Prindy
survives—and about which he himself is completely reticent, feign-
ing amnesia or even imbecility to fool the whites. And there is the
same conspicuous reluctance to pass judgment on the protagonists.

At times, indeed, Herbert seems almost to want to deny causality
altogether. He says at one point, for instance, "But what seem good
works to some may be judged sheer evil by others. The corollary
perhaps is that there is neither good nor evil. The trouble is that
corollaries are the deductions of minds, which is to say, in most if
not all cases, prejudice."[12] Herbert seems here to be in danger of
falling into what Conrad called "a mere, bland indifferentism."
Similarly, he makes a reference much later in the novel to "Sin,
which perhaps is another name for Nature."[13]

But the curious thing is that this tendency to discount moral
responsibility for actions goes hand in hand with an opposed habit
of intervening in the narrative—either through Jeremy or in the
directly authorial voice—to impose judgments of the characters'
actions of the harshest possible kind. If sin is only another word for
nature, nevertheless it remains true that Herbert is quite unmerciful,
as he was in *Soldiers' Women*, upon the sinners.

Continually throughout the narrative there are personal intrusions
in order to make critical remarks about the characters or to insist
that their actions are interpreted in the worst possible light. If the
novel is Tolstoyan in length it is hardly so in charity. Many of these
tiresomely repetitive remarks, of course, are made through the
consciousness and sometimes in the actual voice of Jeremy. In the
space of one, not untypical page, for instance,[14] he can insert
disparaging remarks concerning his son Clancy, white Australians'
rejection of Aboriginal names, their predatory and destructive
hunting habits, the condition of the "poor beaten blacks," the
murderous habits of the white inhabitants of the land towards each
other, and the vast majority of Australians in general (all except
"bush Australians") who, he says, "aren't really Australians at all,
just transplanted Pommies[15] or something equally alien." He is a
man full of bile and bitterness who seems to have a grudge against

mankind because it (and especially its Australian-born representatives) has failed to live up to his own expectations of it.

Of course, all this could be attributed to Jeremy alone, with Herbert not necessarily in agreement with his character, but once again it needs to be insisted that despite the occasional criticisms Herbert makes of his spokesman, passages in the authorial voice are extremely similar both in tone and attitudes to those in which Jeremy's consciousness is being rendered.[16]

Moreover, sometimes what amounts to a deliberate blurring of character and author seems to take place. Consider, for instance, the following passage:

Jeremy removed his coat as he walked the street, causing the passing sweating overclad mob to stare at him as a freak. He went to the Art Gallery. There he had to don the coat again, for a start because the attendant, doubtless thinking he intended to sneak out something wrapped in it, wanted to take it from him, and then because the usually chilly climate of these parts was trapped eternally in the mass of the place. Here again was the sun-loved substance of the land, its granite, torn out to make igloos for the cold-blooded aliens.

Whether because of his mood of the moment, or the fact that the pictures of battle were the biggest and most spectacular and he no connoisseur of art, he gave most of his attention to these. Surely the artists who had painted them had never seen actual warfare, since even while exposing homicidal mania with skilful depiction of facial expression, they showed nothing of the filthy reality: the burst intestines, clotted severed limbs, agony so frightful that there could be none of the final courage implied by the nobility of the faces of the dead. Maybe true artists don't go to war, or going, don't return. Maybe you couldn't get your picture hung in an art gallery if you painted the truth. That seemed to be what Jeremy was thinking, as, with quizzical expression, he went from one handsome lie to another.[17]

It is difficult, I think, to argue that this is not a petulant piece of writing, particularly in the first paragraph with its constant carping at city people and city habits. (As in *Soldiers' Women*, his animus against city life seems to bring out a great deal of Herbert's worst writing.) What is significant, however, is the equivocation— "Whether because of . . .," "Surely," "Maybe," "That seemed to be what Jeremy was thinking . . ."—in deciding exactly whose irritations are being aired. Is Jeremy's neurotic reaction to the crowd presented as being a product of his paranoia or is Herbert not, rather, in fairly complete sympathy with it but unwilling to declare himself openly, or confused in his sympathies—hence the profession of ignorance?

From the rest of the urban section—with its innumerable references to city dwellers as ants or insects—I do not think there can be much doubt about the answer. Despite the evidence of the omniscient point of view so that, for instance, the novelist can report Prindy's singing in his sleep when no other character is present, the prose is qualified constantly by phrases such as those I pointed to in the passage quoted.

Disclaimers such as "Perhaps," "with an expression that seemed to suggest," "a female, who by her expression," "Whether it was Aboriginal wariness," all suggestive of the author's self-imposed limitation of knowledge and externality of observation, abound in the novel but never more often than when Jeremy is the object of its attention. Is it unfair to suggest that Herbert wishes to have Jeremy's views accepted as those of himself yet to evade the responsibility of accepting the man's most jingoistic excesses— as if his instincts as a novelist and craftsman are at war with his impulse to indulge all his most treasured bigotries?

It is an issue that is central to any final evaluation of the novel because despite the frequent *ad hominem* interventions and what one could call the diffident omniscience of the point of view of the novel it seems clear that we are asked to admire Jeremy deeply and to see many of the positions he adopts as ones worthy of emulation, and if we cannot do this then a great deal of the novel simply defies credibility. The "willing suspension of disbelief" of which Coleridge speaks becomes impossible.

The qualities invested in Jeremy, and the flatteries bestowed upon him are finally not merely incredible but offensive. In the far too long and almost completely redundant opening dialogue (virtually monologue) between Jeremy and Bishoff the stock inspector regards him almost with veneration and interrupts his discourse only to make such flattering remarks as "But please go on. I find everything you say quite fascinating. It gives a new slant to things I'd taken for granted."[18] This is immediately after Jeremy has quite rudely and gratuitously described him as a silvertail, one of his most frequent terms of abuse. Herbert constantly insists upon Jeremy's physical charms: after declaring her love for him, Lydia spends a "moment of staring at his dim-lit profile, the craggy manly beauty of it."[19] A year later, when Alfie similarly sets out unsuccessfully to seduce him Herbert observes: "Yet again did Jeremy tell his bitter tale to a female, who by her expression, was listening as much to the deep male music of his voice as to his words."[20] Later, she ponders, "It was exciting, to walk the streets with that stance of Nobleness and Excellence, beside the big man who carried those qualities so well, so that every head turned to look."[21]

Jeremy manages to satisfy both Bridie and Alfie sexually where their respective husbands in contrast seem almost impotent. Nan regards herself as his slave while he seems, as far as we can tell, to respond to Rifkah's early love for him but to refrain from expressing it carnally because of Esk's warnings that he is virtually *in loco parentis* to her; he is, as Herbert puts it later in the book "father and lover combined to perfection in the one man."[22]

Amongst the men, Bishoff is not the only one to see special virtues in Jeremy. Fergus, described early as "a fellow who would come at anything for money,"[23] is morally elevated under Jeremy's quasi parental role during the course of the novel—in pretty much the same proportion that Alfie loses her original freshness and idealism—until near the end he can speculate wistfully, leaving the thought unfinished, "We've got pretty close lately. If I'd had a father like you . . ."[24] Billy Brew hails him as countryman, the novel's highest accolade, after Jeremy confesses to experiencing the apparition of the *Yalmaru*. Even Silas Tripconny, who hardly knows him, says admiringly, "I've never had your masculine strength and integrity."[25] But without doubt, the most astonishingly sycophantic figure is the English general Esk who regards Jeremy as "the one just man in Sodom," a phrase he uses repeatedly and with considerable relish, and who addresses him in terms such as these: " . . . and then yourself, so calm, so casual, impudent if you like, but so much in command of the situation, a man of strength and integrity and even humour."[26]

In one of his many encomiums, Esk tells Jeremy, "If only all Australians were like you, dear boy."[27] But the plain truth—which Herbert is certainly incapable of recognizing—is that if all Australians were like Jeremy life here would be intolerable. For all his celebrated qualities, Jeremy is also a deeply flawed man, an overbearingly righteous, literalminded boor who can accommodate himself for the most part only to people to whom he can feel in some way superior—the blacks, the crippled, those in some way vulnerable and in need of his protection. He is simply incapable of standing as the figure of moral authority that the author wants him to be.

He is also a deeply xenophobic and chauvinistic man who consistently demeans the motives for conduct of the people around him. If his list of accomplishments and qualities is impressive, so too is his list of hatreds and prejudices. He feels varying degrees of hostility towards: the police, the army and its associated rituals of uniforms, the RSL clubs and the celebration of Anzac Day, the upper class ("silvertails"), academics, Nazis, Communists and indeed followers of ideologies of any kind, Aboriginal Protectors and missionaries, homosexuals of both sexes, political leaders of any persuasion (the unnamed Labor Party leader John Curtin is dealt with as severely as the conservative Menzies—also unnamed—and almost as severely as Hughes, Churchill and MacArthur, possibly on the confessed ground that the liking for and pursuit of power is itself an infallible sign of corruption which takes Lord Acton's famous dictum a little further), Christians, gamblers, people who can't hold their liquor or who get drunk regularly, and anyone in any position of service to his fellow human beings whatsoever.

Additionally, among his more esoteric and surprising dislikes are fat people (They've "usually got a mean streak in 'em")[28] and, inexplicably given his feelings about soldiers in general, undersized men in uniform ("Not a warrior-type among them, and ｊｔ undersized," Jeremy comments disapprovingly of his fellow ｏｌ- diers;[29] he has a particular hatred of Dr. Cootes's idol Napoleon, partly on this ground.) There remain two further, more general areas in which Jeremy's set of prejudices repay examination and these deserve special analysis.

V   Jeremy and Women

The first of these is women. Jeremy's attitude towards women— and once again I can find no marked evidence for authorial dissociation from it—is one of a benign protectiveness, what used to be called gallantry, towards an unmistakeably weaker and inferior species. Both the novel's main characters—Jeremy and Prindy— have firm ideas on the place of women in society and are not slow in acting upon them. After he marries his teenage betrothed Savitra, Prindy calmly beats her whenever she is disobedient or complains of being tired; and this action is accepted with equanimity, if not outright approval, by Jeremy and the other characters present. The author himself comments, in speaking of the trouble that flares between the young husband and wife, "But there was the white shrew as well as the docile Indian and the slave-rebel lubra in the little lady,"[30] and the implicit disapproval of her conduct prepares us for her role in her own later appalling tragedy. As for Jeremy, his attitudes towards women can be most easily gauged from the steady stream of aphorisms he issues throughout the novel regarding women and their nature and function that collectively amount to one of the most astonishing examples of the double standard of judgment imaginable.

Among the choicest of his Jeremiads are the following: "It's my philosophy that a man should excuse a woman for just about anything";[31] "A man's love of woman should be a passing thing. Only stupid men remain enthralled by women";[32] "A lady should never get drunk without a reliable male escort . . . and a man never without dignity";[33] "Only a woman knows how to deal with a crying woman . . . the same as with crying children. Women and children cry for many things . . . it can even be from temper or artfulness. Men don't know. They can only guess";[34] "Emasculating the male is the female's business";[35] ". . . the unreliability of women in keeping other's secrets is proverbial";[36] "A man's only happy when he's pursuing a mad idea of a bad woman";[37] and, finally, my own choice, "Women are all the same in the dark."![38]

Jeremy says of Aboriginal initiation ceremony, "Women must be left out of it, because their part in cultural activity is only background . . . which I suppose you could say of most women in all societies, anyhow."[39] The author, in apparent sympathy, speaks at one point of "a whole bevy of females who had the look of having their minds on higher things than most women."[40] The curious thing is that despite all this, Herbert persists in thinking of the black and white societies as matrilineal, a word he employs several times. At one point Jeremy argues reasonably enough that the early whites should have crossbred with the blacks in a more open and decent way than in fact they did and created a Creole nation; but considerably less reasonably that the reason they didn't was that Australian men are dominated by their wives, unlike the South Americans with whom he makes a comparison, and hence were forced to break up their potentially worthwhile liaisons with black women.

Only once in the novel does he seem to me to show an awareness of the real difficulties a women suffers often in the male-female relationship and this is when he replies briefly, in response to Fergus's suggestion that most women are "distorted" by saying that "I think mainly only in so far as the male distorts her. She'd be all right, but for the brutal weakness of the average male. She trades on it. She has to."[41] This is at least a qualification, though not much of one, of the nonsense Jeremy usually speaks about women.

I do not think one has to be a radical feminist or a deeply committed member of women's liberation to find the sort of statements quoted above deeply offensive, and yet, inevitably, the women in the novel are shown to be irresistibly attracted towards the author of them (in accordance with the well-known notion, of course, that women are masochistic and like to be dominated). Lydia, for instance, first surrenders to the impact of Jeremy's charm when he describes her utterly without provocation as "a spoilt child of a system of society I have only contempt for."[42] Inevitably, like most of the characters at some point in the novel, she turns red in anger. Jeremy's sexual potency has already been spoken of, and in fact Herbert several times contrasts pointedly his sexual proficiency in satisfying his various partners with the failures of their own spouses to do so: Bridie's husband, for instance, is impotent and Jeremy has to father the son she wants for her, though her husband believes fondly that it is his. Alfie's husband manages a little better than this but nevertheless leaves his wife unsatisfied and weeping.

More pervasively, the sexual act itself is spoken of as being primarily for woman's satisfaction. Herbert speaks of Savitra being "served" by Prindy in describing their lovemaking[43] and a moment later of her "waking hungry, as any healthy female should from fulfilment of her function." Jeremy (and Herbert seems to follow him in this as well) seems genuinely to believe, in a discussion with Fergus, that sexual indulgence on the part of the male is somehow bound up with adolescent arrest of development and maturity in intellectual and personal ways.

There remains one further unpleasant form of discrimination against women of a different kind, one that suggests again the identity of Jeremy's and Herbert's views, and this is in the peculiar preoccupation the author has with the female urinary processes. He says of Lydia, for instance, that "She pulled her pants down, squatted, gave the parched earth a drink such as it never had before" and then "smirked at his (Jeremy's) evident embarrassment."[44] A page later she is described as "smirking" again as she urinated (the euphemisms for which process that Herbert employs being "pee" and "piddle"). Bridie is described in similar detail performing the same function: "She hitched up her dress, pulled down her drawers, squatted, piddled voluminously as a mare."[45] No explanation is given for these detailed descriptions, which have about them something of Swift's obsession with Celia, and Herbert pays no comparable attention to the males' bodily functions in the novel.

VI *Jeremy and Racism*

Jeremy is a chauvinist in the sense that female radicals have now appropriated the term; but he is also a chauvinist in the sense that the word used to mean. The only reason why women need not feel more violently discriminated against than they otherwise might is that Herbert's disaffection, as expressed through his most important and voluble character, extends to most of the males in the novel. He is not, finally and merely, a misogynist but a misanthropist as well. The only difference is that the forms of hostility towards women that he depicts are the most aggressive and violent in the novel, at least at their worst.

At both the beginning and near the end of the novel horrifying incidents are described in which women who accidentally stumble on male Aboriginal initiation ceremonies have their legs and arms broken, are pack raped by all the males present, and have their breasts and pudenda carved out, roasted, and eaten. These incidents are described in a tone that is not at all indicative of sympathy for the victims but merely dispassionate and neutral, and the Aboriginal culture that includes this custom is spoken of throughout the novel in unequivocally laudatory tones; it is the barbarous whites who intervene and destroy it who are condemned.

I am not, of course, suggesting that Herbert approves of these atrocities but merely that his own double standard—in the matters of both whites versus blacks and men versus women—leads him to be far harder on his own culture, for which he feels a strong sense of guilt and responsibility, than an alien one with its own unacknowledged imperfections. Although he at one stage speaks of the black tracker Jinbull as Cahoon's henchman the ironical thing is that his strictures of the blacks who join against their own kind never lead him to the possible thought that blacks might not be the vastly and intrinsically superior race to the whites he suggests they are, but instead, merely human like us. Virtue and vice surely are not confined exclusively to a single race or people; they will be found universally, mingled in different proportions, or perhaps more accurately, manifested in different forms; and the tragic thing is that in his admirable and perfectly justified sense of outrage at white mistreatment of blacks, the author has been led into so violently overstating and distorting his case that it loses much of its authority.

Jeremy's hatred of other races is so intense and their total is so many that finally it transcends mere xenophobia altogether and becomes a hatred of mankind. The author nowhere appears to dissociate himself from any of these views and indeed adds many similar ones in his own voice. There is scarcely a race that does not at some stage come in for his disapproval.

Thus, the "Chinese-man" is described as an even worse despoiler of the land than the white man. The Japanese are shown as treacherous and described in clichéd terms of their repeatedly hissing and bowing. The Americans are described with similar repetition as materialistic and rapacious. The Germans are said to be the worst of all the migrant groups to have come to Australia because they, as well as "so-called New Australians of Mediterranean and Balkan types who weren't so fussy about what they ate,"[46] kill and sometimes eat the kookaburras. The Italians are also despoilers of the land: "even Wops, neglecting their weekend ring-barking, blasting, ploughing, and otherwise contributing to the making of another Sahara, as their ancestors had so long ago."[47] The "Indian mind" is described as having been "contaminated for so long from Ghengis Khan to Queen Victoria."[48] He speaks of the "Irish prodigality of Finnucane's lights and the Scottish meanness of McDodd's,"[49] thereby managing neatly to insult two more races on precisely opposed grounds. The statements made about the migrants, arguably the best thing that has happened to Australia since the war, are probably the most offensive of all, and many of them are made in the authorial voice. Herbert describes them, for instance, as "those lowest class people in the world, whose own countries were glad to get rid of, the Immigrants."[50]

But the most lavish scorn of all is, of course, reserved for Herbert's own people, the native-born Australians. Examples are innumerable, too many to be listed, but at various points in the novel the author accuses Australians of servility and sycophancy, class distinction, lack of hospitality, intellectual shallowness ("facile as the Australian mind"),[51] having no real sense of humor, being generally obscene, displaying "a deep feeling of inferiority mingled with resent ment,"[52] having a weakness for foreigners of wealth or rank or note, never having had freedom or aspiring towards it, and chronic alcoholism.

There is enormous pain, of course, in these accusations. As Esk remarks to Jeremy, "How you love to malign what you really love so well!"[53] and clearly the very intensity of the feeling arises from the intensity of disappointment at the country having failed to live up to its original promise and potential. Nevertheless the manner in which this feeling expresses itself is most often mean-minded and egotistical.

Moreover, as so often happens, xenophobic bigotry goes hand in hand with innate confusion and contradictoriness of thought. For instance, Jeremy can never quite make up his mind whether to be proud of Australia, and to accept the fact of it as it is now, or to renounce it as stolen property. He speaks of "the selling of our birthright, if you can call inherited stolen property that"[54] and the qualification perfectly expresses his uncertainty. He says of the Aborigines that "Even those few people truly sympathetic towards them think of them as lowly creatures to be raised to our exalted way of life"[55] yet his own thinking about them is by no means free from paternalism. Nan is his self-admitted slave and the only blacks who seem free from a dependent relationship with him are Bobwir-ridirridi and Prindy, whose virtues border on the miraculous and godlike.

He advocates at some length open mixed breeding between whites and blacks[56] in order to combine the best qualities of both, yet throughout the novel shows repeated contempt for half-breeds and those of mixed blood of various kinds. For instance, he comments of one woman that "She was only one quarter white, but possessed of all the potential volcanic violence that seethes in most crossbreeds with white blood."[57] He expresses repeated hatred of the former Australian Prime Minister Billy Hughes on the grounds that he is a Cockney (and in fact castigates Cockneys in general on several occasions). And of all the accusations that one could have brought against Sir Winston Churchill the only one Herbert seizes on is that the man was not a true Englishman but half American!

Jeremy's confusions extend further and it is instructive to observe what happens when one prejudice runs counter to another. For example, he admires Jews enormously (although more after meeting Rifkah than before, if his somewhat perfunctory rebuttal of Bishoff's antiSemitism early in the novel can be taken as representative) and admires xenophobic nationalists but detests Communism, which he defines at one point as "a persuasion made up only of rogues, fools, and madmen, surely, since it aspired to establish the Millenium on a basic tenet of *End Justifies Means*, the philosophy of a common criminal."[58] His portrayals of Pat Hannaford who is a nationalistic Communist, and the group of Communist Jews whom he puts up at his station for a while, therefore, are classic studies in uncertainty and contradiction. The Jewish visitors are described in racist stereotypes, the other side of the same excessive idealism with which he treats Rifkah simply because she is Jewish: "They were big and small, plump, lean, dark, fair, grey, bald, with eyes black, brown, hazel, blue, yet with a resemblance, something hard to define."[59] They never really come alive as characters and one is not sure what one's response to them is quite supposed to be, except that they all, even the likeable Kurt, seem vaguely sinister.

As for Pat, he seems to me, if one takes into account simply his actions as they are described, as generous and idealistic a character as any in the novel, and even to satisfy many of Herbert's criteria for the ideal Australian, and yet the tone of the novel does its best to convey otherwise. He is intensely nationalistic, he fights bravely for his country, he does his best to protect both the Jewish Rifkah and the Aborigines (although, as Herbert correctly points out, he is prone to be patronizing with the latter) and he is the very opposite of sycophantic, taking on the bosses continually. Towards the end, the book's attitude does seem to soften towards him but for most of the time any decent action he undertakes is described in as demeaning and grudging way as possible.

VII   *The Novelist's Perspective*

It is here—in this gap between what the action shows us and the interpretation Herbert attempts to impose upon his material—that one accounts for a great deal of the unsatisfactoriness of the novel. It is central to both the author's desire to portray Jeremy as all the things he patently is not, and the bitterness and malice with which most of the other characters are treated.

There is throughout the novel a positively ingenious straining to avoid the possibility of having to ascribe a generous motive to most of the characters' actions. There are many minor examples. For instance, when Dr. McQuegg shows kindness to the prisoners in his custody Herbert cannot allow it to go unquestioned and adds ambiguously, "Perhaps he was being considerate of the one or two nurses only who would be on duty at the Hospital that night because of the partying."[60] He seems to be as critical of Nugget Knowles's timid restraint with Nell as he is of Nobby's raping of her. But perhaps the point may be made more clearly if we take as examples two fairly important characters who seem to arouse the particular malice of the author and whose conduct, considered as objectively as the novel allows us, seems to contain very little cause for the abuse the author heaps on them.

The treatment of Shamus Finnucane, whom the author detests, apparently on the grounds that he is Irish, is representative of that of many of the aliens in the novel. Despite his blandness and interest in money he is really quite a decent and far from unworthy human being, but one comes to this conclusion only *despite* the tone and inference of most of the writing. His faults seem to be venial at most but Herbert seizes with malicious glee on anything at all that could be made to appear critical of him. Even in the opening account on p. 71 his "always excessive sentiments" are mentioned and he is described as greeting people with "the joy of a man who loved money." Herbert continually derides his accent and the shameful fact of his not having been born in Australia: "old Shame-on-us himself-himself . . . in a gathering largely Irish at least at second-hand."[61] Jeremy is deeply critical of him for not being as rabidly xenophobic about the English as himself and for feeling a deep sense of ambivalence at the prospect of Ireland profiting from the German assault on England, surely a natural enough response for someone in Finnucane's position.

The criticisms extend even to his family. His mother is spoken of as having the bony bitter face of the Irish shrew—another of Herbert's grossly simplistic generalizations—and his sons-in-law, whose fault seems to be that they actually work as his paid employees, are described constantly as imported slave sons-in-law and minions. Their physical appearance is similarly unattractive: they are "ruddy as himself from sun that would ever be alien to them."[62] In the incident of the humiliation of Priddy and Rifkah, especially, when Priddy is turned out of a bar on account of his skin, Finnucane behaves with real tact and courtesy; but this is hardly conceded by either Jeremy or the author, who merely makes a grudging remark about his cunning.

The second notable instance of his malicious treatment of a character is Fay McFee, the objection in this case being her implicit lesbianism (there is no evidence that she actually goes to bed with other women though plenty that she wants to). Herbert's contempt for homosexuals is intense (he speaks continually of Denzil's hysteria and homosexuality, apparently regarding them as comparable maladies) and although Fay is by no means a sympathetic figure the superfluous and gratuitous malice with which he describes her actions are of astonishing proportions.

She is continually spoken of, for instance, even more than the other characters, in animalistic terms, especially feral ones: lines such as "For answer Miss McFee bared her teeth at him and stalked away"[63] are common in the novel. After repeatedly mentioning her baring her teeth he calls her an "inverted virgin"[64] just as the castrated Kurt is a "sexless Socrates."[65] Not content with the metaphors of wolves, the author refers to the "crude reality of the domestic politics in which she had to root for a living like a pig" and a few lines later speaks of "that mass of human female flesh wallowing and puffing like a pink and white buffalo" and of her "bovine sigh."[66] All her reforming journalism, which seems motivated by genuine enough impulses, is described merely as fodder for the sensation-hungry Southern press; and of one piece of journalism in which she was justifiably critical of the outrageous conduct of some of the missionary men, he merely notes grudgingly that "It was too carefully worded for legal repercussions, Fay having sheer genius for libel without action."[67] The author scores off her to the last. Even dead she is described as "a plump figure in male attire."[68]

Both the author and his main character are continually critical of the lesser beings around them, yet Jeremy himself is full of preening righteousness. He says pompously that he has trained himself "in the habit of only two meals a day."[69] Even his drinking is different from that of all the other characters, which is described in almost Dantean terms: " . . . because such thirst as theirs, the Great Australian Thirst, is soul-deep like the thirst of the damned in Hell; the thirst of people with a woeful past and naught but woe for the future."[70] Jeremy, on the other hand, says smugly of himself, "I see alcohol as the most harmless of all the drugs used to physic a congenitally sick species . . . and use it, I think, to its best effect."[71] He also makes the extraordinary claim that brandy, which is all he drinks, "doesn't impair the wits like most other alcoholic beverages."[72]

It is only in the very late stages of the novel that Jeremy begins to lose some of his overwhelming selfrighteousness and show a dim awareness of the possibilities of complexity in human nature. Speaking to his wife about the death of a policeman and one of his colleagues' grief, he says in genuine bewilderment, "Ballywick's almost crying. It's just too much of a bloody puzzle . . . their humanity and inhumanity all mixed up together."[73] This profound discovery—that people are not usually wholly good or wholly bad— leads him in the later stages of the novel to be a little less dogmatic and absolutist in his dealings with his fellow men; he shows, for instance, a certain limited, reluctant gentleness towards old Finnucane in his distress. However, it also has a curiously debilitating effect on him. Shorn of his sustaining dogmatism and selfrighteousness he loses much of his strength and capacity for leadership.

It is the failure of Jeremy as a figure who can authoritatively embody the novel's central insights that is at the heart of its weaknesses. Although there are other important and sympathetic characters who are more convincingly rendered, it is Jeremy who appears to be the author's spokesman on so many issues—and this is a novel full of ideas that are expounded rather than dramatized or embodied in the experience of the novel.

It is simply impossible for the reader to find in Jeremy the example of the perfect Australian that the author—at least until near the end—seems to think him. At the same time as we are presented with the man's ardent love of the land, his resourcefulness, his authority as father figure and lover, we are presented also (apparently unwittingly) with his penchant for juvenile practical jokes, his stuffy complacency, his literalmindedness and all the meaner and ungenerous aspects of his chauvinism and his sexism. There is finally and most incredibly of all the extraordinary ingenuousness of his belief that one can join a fascist movement and ignore or eliminate everything that is fascist about it—and yet Herbert, by the heading of section two and the absence of any qualification of Jeremy's sense of martyrdom after he has been betrayed, seems to ask us to sympathize with the man and his "ideal."

Jeremy is an extremely bitter man, and his bitterness very much pervades the novel, but it is very significant that the nastiness and misanthropy of the tone in which he speaks are just as much present in the scenes in which he does not appear: they belong to the novel as a whole. Even when he is speaking of characters of whom he approves or describing scenes where some kind of tenderness of feeling seems to be aimed at, Herbert cannot refrain from employing dehumanizing or derogatory language.

There are two stylistic traits in particular that one can point to as emphasizing the misanthropic tone that pervades the whole novel.

The first, which we saw in the example of Fay McFee, is the bestowing of animalistic features on human beings. Animalistic terms are applied to both men and women, almost invariably when seen *en masse* (in the cities, for example), or doing anything physical such as eating or making love.

The characters' hands are frequently described as claws. Nell's cockatoo screech has already been mentioned. Piggy Trotter inevitably is described in terms of his porcine habits and features, as is the warden at the jail where Jeremy is kept. Turkney shows his teeth and snarls. Mr. Dorcas is shown "breathing like a stranded dugong," and a moment later exposes "the outlines of a prodigious arse and what must have been veritable pack-bags of testicles dangling between his legs."[74] Crowds are described as being "like bluebottles on a carcass"[75] and "swarming over flies like dung."[76] There are innumerable other examples but the point is clear enough.

The obverse of this is, of course, the elevation of animals to a status higher than that of human beings. Herbert several times characterizes men as inferior to horses, and General Esk speaks of the horse as "what, after all, is a nobler animal than man generally."[77]

The second, and related, stylistic habit, one that is finally perhaps even more destructive to one's respect for the characters than the first, is the application of grossly physical and nauseating terms to the most mundane and inoffensive of activities. People in this novel do not laugh as often as they cackle; they do not drink but guzzle and do not eat but hog. They pant, rather than breathe, and blubber or whimper or snivel, rather than merely crying. Most often of all they grunt inarticulately and Herbert continually and with contempt renders these sounds phonetically in order to make the perpetrater seem as absurd as possible. Conversations are frequently punctuated by "arrrh" or "eeeeahhh!" or variations on these, so that the speaker seems hardly to have advanced beyond the simian stage. When Father Glascock makes love to Rifkah Herbert conveys the passion of the occasion with "He panted and slobbered."[78] And finally, as I mentioned earlier, there are those preposterous accents.

VIII   *The Style of the Novel*

There remains a final criticism, one that has been already adumbrated in the previous section, and that is the sheer ineptitude of the writing at a local level, irrespective of the overall scheme of the novel. It is not merely the whole slipshod, careless presentation of the book: for instance, there are something over five hundred proof reading errors, at one stage we jump from section one to section three, and one character changes name from Mrs. March to Mrs. Marsh during the course of the novel for no apparent reason. But the style in general is stuffed with clichés.

Smirks are often flung in this novel. Similarly, brows rumple, faces burn, redden, glow, or flush while the character simultaneously exhales, and more rarely one of the characters might turn pale. Glances are also flung or sometimes merely exchanged, people heave with feeling or draw deep breaths, eye each other searchingly and exchange smiles, and males stab kisses at females.

Herbert is unremittingly conscientious in describing the details of every one of the characters' eyes and the various actions and movements between and among them. For instance, when the three Delacys and the new stock inspector Bishoff are introduced from the perspective of the young boy Prindy, it is in terms almost solely of their eyes: "There were three pairs of light eyes, two blue, one grey and exactly like his own, the fourth greenish in a very red face as the sweat-streaks showed."[79] Eyes in the novel lock together, or hold other eyes. "So many eyes leaping to challenge the grey eyes," Herbert writes at one point, "blue eyes, green, grey, brown, black—and the grey widening to meet them but never flinching."[80] In this world of busy oracular collisions, characters eye each other searchingly, eyes are dragged from the sea or sometimes snap at a character; sometimes they merely drop or fall, but they also have a tendency, under the stress of deep emotion, to pop.

The general woodenness of the writing, the absence of the kind of energy and crackling life of *Capricornia*, is exacerbated by its enormous repetition and overstatement. Jeremy's long opening harangue to Bishoff is followed by another long one to Lydia[81] in which substantially the same ideas are repeated. Alfie's book is virtually a restatement of much of this one, a novel within a novel, with a slight shift of emphasis and fascist intonation which *Poor Fellow My Country* itself does not share.

Irony works best, as a rule, when it is understated; in this novel it is bellowed at the reader. Many of the ironic juxtapositions Herbert makes might have worked well. For instance, Herbert comments neatly at one point, "They swung round the cemeteries. Only two here, European and Asiatic, the latter being very large. Aborigines were buried in what was shown on the map of the town as the Sanitary Reserve, also used for the dumping of rubbish."[82] Here the author is content to leave his point to make itself. Far more often, however, he follows it up with a long speech in which the significance of the point is spelled out at tedious length.

Poor Fellow My Country is a very unhappy book to read and even more so to reread. There can be no questioning the sincerity and deep feeling of its intentions, and a great many of its ideas— they remain no more than that for the most part—are admirable, especially when shorn of their more unpleasantly chauvinistic elements. There is no need to reject or refuse to welcome migrants and the very real contribution they have made to the prosperity and cultural achievement of the country in order to resent the imperialistic elements in English and American interests here. There can be no disagreeing with Herbert's passionate feeling of shame at white Australians' treatment of the blacks whose land they have expropriated. And many Australians apart from myself might well agree with his diagnosis of ours as an unspiritual, aimless, materialistic society. But ideas and intentions, even when they are noble, which is not all the time in this novel, do not in themselves make great art, and one only wishes that Herbert had subjected his giant novel to a far more ruthless editing and revision so that the real novel that is buried somewhere inside the book could have emerged.

As it is, I believe its status in the country's national literature will in the years to come be primarily that of a curiosity, a kind of literary brontosaurus, *Poor Bugger My Book*. It is an unhappy conclusion to a long, distinguished, and courageous career.

Notes and References

and

Selected Bibliography

Notes and References

Chapter One

1. Camden Morrisby, "Xavier Herbert and the World He Knows," *Australasian Book News and Literary Journal*, I, no. 2, (1946), 43.
2. Jillian Robertson, "Not For Delicate People," *The Bulletin*, October 19, 1963, p. 25.
3. A. D. Hope, "Australia" in his *Collected Poems, 1930-1970*, Sydney: Angus & Robertson, 1972, p. 13. Outsiders interested in Australia can gain an extremely useful introduction to the country from this scathing but astute poem.
4. From Xavier Herbert's letters in the National Library, Canberra. MS 758, Series III.
5. Furnley Maurice, "The Literary Value of Human Agony," *The Australian Quarterly*, 10, no. 2, June, 1938, 65.
6. Vincent Buckley, "*Capricornia*," *Meanjin*, XIX (1960), 13-30.
7. Letter to Dr. J. B. Beston, September 10, 1972. National Library, Canberra.
8. John Hetherington, *Forty-Two Faces* (Melbourne, 1962), p. 48.
9. Patricia Rolfe, " 'Old 'Orrible' Loves Australia," *The Bulletin*, January 5, 1974, p. 33.
10. Quoted in Hetherington, Op. cit., p. 51.
11. Brian Kiernan, "Testing Dreams Against Reality," *The Age*, September 13, 1975, p. 19.
12. Edward Kynaston, "Flawed Achievement," *Overland* No. 62, pp. 76-78.
13. Don Grant, "Xavier Herbert's Botch," *Overland* No. 65 (1976), pp. 43-47.
14. Laurie Hergenhan, "Rebuttal: a Defence of Xavier Herbert's *Poor Fellow My Country*", *Overland* No. 67, pp. 41-42.
15. Geoffrey Dutton, "Literary View", *The Weekend Australian*, April 29-30, 1978, p. 8.

Chapter Two

1. Xavier Herbert, "Autobiographette," *The Publicist*, 24, June 1, 1938, 9.
2. Xavier Herbert, *Disturbing Element* (Melbourne, 1963), p. 11.

3. Ibid., p. 19.

4. Ibid., p. 21.

5. Ibid., p. 26.

6. Xavier Herbert, "My Thousandth Death," *Quadrant*, VIII, no. 1 (1964), 43.

7. Herbert, *Disturbing Element*, p. 1.

8. Ibid., p. 47.

9. Herbert, "Autobiographette," p. 9.

10. Herbert, *Disturbing Element*, p. 104.

11. Ibid., p. 104.

12. Ibid., p. 104.

13. Xavier Herbert, "I Sinned Against Syntax," *Meanjin*, XIX (1960), 33.

14. Xavier Herbert, "I, the Little Widow, and the World," *Meanjin*, Op. cit., 36-48. This was part of a special issue of *Meanjin* devoted to the work of Herbert.

15. Herbert, *Disturbing Element*, p. 115.

16. Ibid., p. 133.

17. Ibid., p. 174.

18. Ibid., p. 153.

19. Ibid., p. 200.

20. Ibid., p. 267.

21. Hetherington, *Forty-Two Faces*, p. 52.

22. Herbert, "Autobiographette," p. 9.

23. Herbert, *Disturbing Element*, p. 230.

24. Camden Morrisby, "Xavier Herbert and the World He Knows," *Australasian Book News and Literary Journal*, I, no. 2 (1946), 43.

25. Patricia Rolfe, Op. cit., p. 33.

26. Xavier Herbert, "The Writing of *Capricornia*," *Australian Literary Studies*, IV (1970), pp. 207-14.

27. Xavier Herbert, "How *Capricornia* Was Made," *The Bulletin*, March 8, 1961, p. 51.

28. Camden Morrisby, Op. cit., p. 42.

29. See, for instance, his "A Reasoned Case Against Semitism," *The Australian Quarterly*, XII, no. I, March, 1940, 52-62.

30. Xavier Herbert, "Herbert's Retort to Stephensen," *The Bulletin*, March 29, 1961, p. 52.

31. Herbert, "The Writing of *Capricornia*," p. 214.

32. Ibid., p. 213. For further light on this quarrel see Ian Reid, "A Splendid Bubble: Publishing and Fiction-Writing in the 'Thirties," *Meanjin Quarterly*, 33, (1974), 266-71.

33. See, for instance, "*Capricornia*: Some First and Last Impressions of a Great Australian Novel," *The Publicist*, February 1, 1938, pp. 5-7.

34. Herbert, "How *Capricornia* Was Made," p. 52.

35. Herbert, "I Sinned Against Syntax," p. 31.

36. Ibid., p. 35.
37. Ibid., p. 34.
38. Harry Heseltine, *Xavier Herbert* (Melbourne: Oxford University Press, 1973), p. 21.
39. Herbert, "I Sinned Against Syntax," p. 35.
40. Xavier Herbert, "The Signing of the Peace Treaty," *The Australian*, March 29, 1975.

Chapter Three

1. See, for instance, the article quoted earlier by Furnley Maurice, who implicitly compares the novel to the "great and gloomy Russians." It is a comparison which will be much more consciously employed when *Poor Fellow My Country* is published.
2. Xavier Herbert, *Capricornia* (Sydney, 1938), p.1. Page references are to the paperback edition published by Angus & Robertson, Sydney, 1972.
3. Ibid., p. 3.
4. Ibid., p. 155.
5. Ibid., p. 35.
6. Ibid., p. 113.
7. Ibid., p. 259.
8. Ibid., p. 260.
9. Ibid., p. 270.
10. Ibid., p. 2.
11. Ibid., p. 46.
12. Ibid., p. 9.
13. Ibid., p. 176.
14. Ibid., p. 312.
15. Ibid., p. 79.
16. Ibid., p. 82.
17. Ibid., p. 82.
18. Ibid., p. 104.
19. Ibid., p. 177.
20. Ibid., p. 309.
21. Ibid., p. 50.
22. Ibid., p. 55.
23. Ibid., p. 95.
24. Ibid., p. 104.
25. Ibid., p. 165.
26. Laurie Hergenhan, introduction to the paperback edition of *Capricornia*, p. vii.
27. Ibid., p. viii.
28. Herbert, *Capricornia*, pp. 174-75.
29. Harry Heseltine, *Xavier Herbert*, p. 12.
30. Xavier Herbert, *Poor Fellow My Country* (Sydney, 1975), p. 1084.

31. Herbert, *Capricornia*, p. 326.
32. Ibid., p. 46.
33. Ibid., p. 322.
34. Ibid., pp. 69-75.
35. Ibid., p. 282.
36. Ibid., p. 286.
37. Ibid., p. 293.
38. Ibid., p. 260.
39. Ibid., p. 441.
40. Ibid., p. 174.
41. Ibid., p. 34.
42. Ibid., p. 134.
43. Ibid., p. 34.
44. Ibid., p. 47.
45. Ibid., p. 210.
46. Ibid., p. 215.
47. Brian Kiernan, "Xavier Herbert: *Capricornia*," *Australian Literary Studies*, IV (1970), 361. This essay was later reprinted in Kiernan's *Images of Society and Nature: Seven Australian Novels* (Melbourne, 1971).

Chapter Four

1. Herbert, "I Sinned Against Syntax," pp. 34-35.
2. Ibid., p. 34.
3. Xavier Herbert, *Seven Emus* (Sydney, 1959), p. 5.
4. Ibid., p. 82.
5. Ibid., p. 5.
6. Ibid., p. 12.
7. Ibid., p. 16.
8. Ibid., p. 57.
9. Ibid., p. 112.
10. Ibid., p. 87.
11. Ibid., p. 13.
12. Ibid., p. 120.
13. Ibid., p. 49.
14. Xavier Herbert, "A Town Like Elliott," *The Bulletin*, March 31, 1962, p. 24.
15. Herbert, *Seven Emus*, p. 86.
16. Ibid., p. 10.
17. Ibid., p. 57.
18. Ibid., p. 16.

Chapter Five

1. Herbert, *Disturbing Element*, p. 144.
2. Xavier Herbert, *Soldiers' Women* (Sydney, 1961), p. 21.
3. Ibid., p. 126.

4. Ibid., p. 142.
5. Ibid., p. 142.
6. Ibid., p. 440.
7. Ibid., p. 427.
8. Ibid., p. 331.
9. Ibid., p. 85.
10. Ibid., p. 166.
11. Ibid., p. 465.
12. Herbert, "I Sinned Against Syntax," p. 32.
13. Herbert, *Soldiers' Women*, p. 102.
14. Ibid., p. 85.
15. Ibid., p. 84.
16. Ibid., p. 90.
17. Ibid., p. 206.
18. Ibid., p. 311.
19. Ibid., p. 312.
20. Ibid., p. 8.
21. Ibid., p. 77.
22. Ibid., p. 123.
23. Ibid., p. 206.
24. Ibid., p. 220.
25. Ibid., p. 222.
26. Ibid., p. 258.
27. Ibid., p. 296.
28. Ibid., p. 324.
29. Ibid., p. 338.
30. Ibid., p. 414.
31. Ibid., p. 152.
32. Ibid., p. 309.
33. Ibid., p. 378.
34. Ibid., p. 104.
35. Ibid., p. 155.
36. Ibid., p. 199.
37. Ibid., p. 230.
38. Ibid., p. 240.
39. Ibid., p. 372.
40. Ibid., p. 314.
41. Ibid., p. 263.
42. Ibid., p. 265.
43. Ibid., p. 99.
44. Ibid., p. 114.
45. Ibid., p. 147.
46. Ibid., p. 191.
47. Ibid., p. 238.
48. Ibid., p. 331.
49. Ibid., p. 393.

50. Ibid., p. 296.
51. Ibid., p. 143.
52. Ibid., p. 40.
53. Ibid., p. 83.
54. Ibid., p. 235.
55. Ibid., p. 282.
56. Ibid., p. 278.
57. Ibid., pp. 437-39.
58. Ibid., p. 423.
59. Ibid., p. 170.
60. Ibid., p. 206.
61. Ibid., p. 211.
62. Ibid., p. 225.
63. Ibid., p. 198.
64. Ibid., p. 48.
65. Ibid., p. 50.
66. Ibid., p. 80.
67. Ibid., p. 436.
68. Ibid., p. 9.
69. Ibid., p. 461.
70. Ibid., p. 113.
71. Ibid., p. 194.
72. Ibid., p. 21.
73. Ibid., p. 380.
74. Ibid., p. 464.

Chapter Six

1. Herbert, *Letters.* MS 758 Series 2.
2. Herbert, Ibid.
3. Herbert, Ibid.
4. Herbert, *Larger Than Life* (Sydney, 1963), p. 59.
5. Ibid., p. 123.
6. Ibid., p. 39.
7. Ibid., p. 128.
8. Ibid., p. 151.
9. Ibid., p. 3.
10. Ibid., p. 1.
11. Ibid., p. 22.
12. Ibid., p. 80.
13. Ibid., p. 54.
14. Ibid., pp. 93-94.
15. Ibid., p. 133.
16. Ibid., p. 203.
17. Heseltine, *Xavier Herbert*, p. 41.

Chapter Seven

1. Xavier Herbert, *Poor Fellow My Country* (Sydney, 1975), p. 589.
2. Ibid., p. 190.
3. Ibid., p. 484.
4. Ibid., p. 692.
5. Ibid., p. 929.
6. Ibid., p. 1310.
7. Ibid., p. 59.
8. Ibid., p. 1184.
9. Ibid., p. 1401.
10. Ibid., p. 1272.
11. Ibid., p. 454.
12. Ibid., p. 265.
13. Ibid., p. 1330.
14. Ibid., p. 109.
15. "Pommie" is Australian slang for "Englishman."
16. They are also strikingly similar to remarks Herbert has made in his own person.
17. Herbert, *Poor Fellow My Country*, p. 1165.
18. Ibid., p. 30.
19. Ibid., p. 151.
20. Ibid., p. 531.
21. Ibid., p. 644.
22. Ibid., p. 1084.
23. Ibid., p. 567.
24. Ibid., p. 1273.
25. Ibid., p. 1057.
26. Ibid., p. 658.
27. Ibid., p. 1164.
28. Ibid., p. 910.
30. Ibid., p. 1314.
31. Ibid., p. 139.
32. Ibid., p. 141.
33. Ibid., p. 146.
34. Ibid., p. 543.
35. Ibid., p. 1296.
36. Ibid., p. 536.
37. Ibid., p. 168.
38. Ibid., p. 487.
39. Ibid., p. 1304.
40. Ibid., p. 231.
41. Ibid., p. 1306.
42. Ibid., p. 106.
43. Ibid., p. 1384.

44. Ibid., p. 157.
45. Ibid., p. 169.
46. Ibid., p. 1452.
47. Ibid., p. 1459.
48. Ibid., p. 475.
49. Ibid., p. 478.
50. Ibid., p. 1396.
51. Ibid., p. 577.
52. Ibid., p. 1127.
53. Ibid., p. 1139.
54. Ibid., p. 37.
55. Ibid., p. 30.
56. Ibid., p. 53.
57. Ibid., p. 39.
58. Ibid., p. 1023.
59. Ibid., p. 797.
60. Ibid., p. 222.
61. Ibid., p. 82.
62. Ibid., p. 72.
63. Ibid., p. 262.
64. Ibid., p. 872.
65. Ibid., p. 872.
66. Ibid., p. 872.
67. Ibid., p. 273.
68. Ibid., p. 1353.
69. Ibid., p. 132.
70. Ibid., p. 489.
71. Ibid., p. 491.
72. Ibid., p. 1023.
73. Ibid., p. 974.
74. Ibid., p. 257.
75. Ibid., p. 88.
76. Ibid., p. 502.
77. Ibid., p. 657.
78. Ibid., p. 1323.
79. Ibid., p. 19.
80. Ibid., p. 256.
81. Ibid., pp. 107-49.
82. Ibid., p. 224.

Selected Bibliography

PRIMARY SOURCES

1. Original Manuscripts

Xavier Herbert's letters are retained in the National Library, Canberra. They include four folders of letters he wrote in the nineteen thirties (undated as to year), his letter to Dr. Beston from which I have quoted, letters to Miles Franklin, and also notebooks he kept later, as well as the original MS of *Soldiers' Women*.

2. Books by Xavier Herbert (In order of publication)

Capricornia. Sydney: Publicist Press, 1938.
Seven Emus. Sydney: Angus & Robertson, 1959.
Soldiers' Women. Sydney: Angus & Robertson, 1961.
Disturbing Element. Melbourne: Cheshire, 1963.
Larger Than Life. Sydney: Angus & Robertson, 1963.
Poor Fellow My Country. Sydney: William Collins, 1975.

3. Stories and Articles by Xavier Herbert (In order of publication)

"Lynch 'Em! Aboriginal 'Crime' in the Northern Territory." *The Publicist*, No. 23, 1 May 1938, p. 2.
"Autobiographette." *The Publicist*, No. 24, 1 June 1938, p. 9.
"I Sinned Against Syntax." *Meanjin* XIX (1960), pp. 31-35.
"I, The Little Widow & The World." *Meanjin* XIX (1960), pp. 36-48.
"The Last Australian." *Meanjin* XIX (1960), pp. 361-66.
"Bang Goes My O.B.E.!" *The Bulletin*, 22 February 1961, p. 52.
"How *Capricornia* Was Made." *The Bulletin*, 8 March 1961, pp. 51-52. Reprinted as "How I Wrote *Capricornia*." *The Observer*, 18 March 1961, pp. 22-23.
"Herbert's Retort to Stephensen." *The Bulletin*, 29 March 1961, p. 52.
"Tom Flynn of Rum Jungle." *The Bulletin*, 31 March 1962, p. 12.
"A Town Like Elliott." *The Bulletin*, 31 March 1962, pp. 23-25.

"The Black Beast." *Literary Review* VII (1963-64), 186-96. Reprinted in
   Quadrant VIII (1964), 43-48 as "My Thousandth Death."
"The Writing of *Capricornia.*" *Australian Literary Studies* IV (1970), 207-
   14.
"The Signing of the Peace Treaty." *The Australian*, 29 March 1975.

SECONDARY SOURCES

BUCKLEY, VINCENT. "*Capricornia.*" *Meanjin*, 19 (1960), 13-30. Also in
   Australian Literary Criticism, ed. Grahame Johnston, pp. 169-86.
   Melbourne: Oxford University Press, 1962. This seminal essay rejects
   the view that *Capricornia* is essentially an example of social realism,
   and subsequent criticism has tended to stress the antirealistic and
   experimental elements in the novel.
CLANCY, LAURIE. "The Design of *Capricornia.*" *Meanjin Quarterly*, 34
   (1975), 150-56. Both this and the article below are earlier versions of
   the appropriate chapters in this book.
———. "*Poor Fellow My Country:* Xavier Herbert's Masterpiece?" *South-
   erly*, 37 (1977), 163-75.
EWERS, JOHN K. *Creative Writing in Australia*. Melbourne: Georgian
   House, 1945. Pp. 88-89. Typical early criticism. Herbert intent on a
   "frank exposure" of the "colour problem in the Northern Territory."
GRANT, DON. "Xavier Herbert's Botch," *Overland*, no. 65 (1976), 43-47.
   An indictment of the "extent and the intensity" of the "polemical
   author's intrusion into his art" in *Poor Fellow My Country*. No direct
   examination of the text.
GREEN, H. M. *A History of Australian Literature*. Sydney: Angus &
   Robertson, 1961. Pp. 1126-30. Qualified emphasis on Herbert's social
   realism.
HADGRAFT, CECIL. *Australian Literature*, London: Heinemann, 1960. Pp.
   256-57. Herbert as social realist and "lightning artist." The social critic
   and commentator who cannot help laughing.
HERGENHAN, LAURIE. "An Australian Tragedy: Xavier Herbert's *Poor
   Fellow My Country*," *Quadrant*, 21 (1977), 62-70. Argues that *Poor
   Fellow My Country* represents a "culminating development in both
   Herbert's own work and in the more recent Australian novel," combin-
   ing and transcending previous forms, i.e., "social realism, the nationalistic (including preoccupation with the land), and spiritual realiza-
   tion."
———. "Rebuttal: A Defence of Xavier Herbert's *Poor Fellow My Coun-
   try*," *Overland*, no. 67, pp. 41-42. Basically a rebuttal of Don Grant's
   dismissal of *Poor Fellow My Country* (see above).
HESELTINE, HARRY. "Australian Fiction Since 1920." In *The Literature of
   Australia*, ed. Geoffrey Dutton, pp. 217-18, 236-37. Melbourne: Pen-

guin, 1976. "With *Capricornia* the Australian novel began to free itself from the limits of external realism."

———. "Xavier Herbert's Magnum Opus," *Meanjin Quarterly*, 34 (1975), 133-36. Describes *Poor Fellow My Country* as "a savage assault on Australia here and now in the timeless work of the imagination."

———. *Xavier Herbert*. Melbourne: Oxford University Press, 1973. Ascribes the imaginative purpose of *Capricornia* (and later works) to Herbert's "deep motive," i.e., "the definition of his own reality against the measure of his father's dominance."

HETHERINGTON, JOHN. *Forty-Two Faces*. Melbourne: Cheshire, 1962. Pp. 48-53. Brief account of personal background of the author and of the critical reception accorded his earlier works.

KELLY, DAVID. "Landscape in *Poor Fellow My Country*." *Overland*, no. 67, pp. 43-46. A critical but not particularly helpful demonstration from *Poor Fellow My Country* of Herbert's "evocation of the land, both in its own right and as an aspect of character and action."

KIERNAN, BRIAN. *Images of Society and Nature: Seven Essays on Australian Novels*. Melbourne: Oxford University Press, 1971. The essay on *Capricornia* is reprinted from *Australian Literary Studies*, 6 (1970), 360-70. Argues for the genuinely experimental nature of *Capricornia:* ". . . the comic distortions of *Capricornia* present us not with a realistic description of any world that exists objectively but with the response to it of an imagination that is passionately involved with the experience it is re-creating."

KYNASTON, EDWARD. "Flawed Achievement." *Overland*, no. 62, pp. 76-78. An energetic demolition job on *Poor Fellow My Country* which "seems to be expressing a strong nationalism based on anger, hatred and violence and finally self pity." Persuasive.

MORRISBY, CAMDEN. "Xavier Herbert and the World He Knows." *Australian Book News*, 1 (1946), 42-43. Personal background.

PONS, XAVIER. "Caste and Castration: The Personal Element in *Capricornia*," *Caliban*, 14 (1977), 133-47. Focuses on one particular element in the novel.

PRICE, CECIL. "Xavier Herbert." *Anglo-Welsh Review*, 26 (1976), 148-53.

PRIDEAUX, HELEN. "The Experimental Novel in Australia: Xavier Herbert's *Capricornia*." *Prospect*, no. 2 (1960), 13-16. "Herbert is an experimental novelist creating a form that is congruous with his social and moral purpose."

REID, IAN. "A Splendid Bubble: Publishing and Fiction—Writing in the 'Thirties.'" *Meanjin Quarterly*, 33 (1974), 266-71. A useful account of the much-disputed history of the editing and publishing of *Capricornia*.

ROBERTSON, JILLIAN, "Not For Delicate People." *The Bulletin*, 19 October 1963, pp. 25-27. Press interview at time of publication of first volume of *Disturbing Element*—almost an Herbertian monologue.

ROBERTSON, ROBERT T. "Form into Shape: *His Natural Life* and *Capricornia* in a Commonwealth Context." In *Commonwealth Literature and the Modern World,* ed. Hena Maes-Jelinek, pp. 137-46. Brussels: Didier, 1975.

STEPHENSEN, P. R. "*Capricornia:* Some First and Last Impressions of a Great Australian Novel." *The Publicist,* no. 20 (1 February 1938), 5-7. A remarkable period piece identifying Herbert as a "realist" whose work is the "Quintessence of Australia." A fascinating demonstration of Australian nationalism rampant.

————. "How I Edited *Capricornia.*" *The Bulletin,* 15 March 1961, pp. 33-34. An idiosyncratic publisher/editor's account of his dealings with the idiosyncratic author.

Index

Angus & Robertson, 38, 39, 41
Austen, Jane, 64
Australian Literary Studies, 35
Australian Journal, 33, 36, 97, 105
Australian, The, 137n4
Australian Quarterly, The 136n2

Beston, J.B. (Dr.), 135n7
Buckley, Vincent, 46, 135n6
Bulletin, The, 136n27, 136n30

Churchill, Winston, 120, 125
Coleridge, S.T., 118
Conrad, Joseph, 116
Cousins, Walter, 38
Curtin, J., 120

Davies, Rhys, 36
Davis, Beatrice, 41
Davidson, Frank Dalby: *The White Thorntree*, 85
Dibley, Arthur, 97
Dickens, Charles, 62, 73
Dutton, Geoffrey, 135n15

Elkin, Professor, 38
Endeavour Press, 37, 38
English Argosy, 99

Fanfrolico Press, 36
Freud, 25, 72
Furphy, Joseph: *Such is Life*, 60, 132

Galsworthy, 98
Guillan, Miss, 26

Hahn, Beverley, 61
Harte, Bret, 67
Henry, O., 98
Herbert, Bill, 25
Herbert, Bridget, 33
Herbert, Horatio, 25

Herbert, Merlin, 28
Herbert, Philip, 23, 25, 28, 32
Herbert, Sadie, 27, 29, 35, 42, 97
Herbert, Victoria, 25
Herbert, Xavier, Aboriginal Protector of Compound in Darwin, 38; attitude to Aborigines, 47-50, 57-60, 64-66, 73-76, 103-104, 109-12, 116, 123-26; attitude to women, 78-85, 86-91, 120-23; Australian Literature Society's Gold Medal, 39; characterization, 56-63; Commonwealth Literary Fund Fellowship, 39; Commonwealth Literary Fund Scholarship, 41; debate over editing of Capricornia, 36-40; fascination with Australian landscape, 24, 34, 49; fights in World War II, 40; marriage, 36; nationalism, 24, 109-12, 113-20, 123-26; political attitudes, 29-32; qualifies as pharmacist, 32; receives Miles Franklin Award, 43; relationship with father, 24-25, 56-57; sexual attitudes, 26-28, 78-84, 85-91; spirit of the land, 74-76; travels to England, 35; wins Sesquicentennial Commonwealth Prize, 39; writes for Smith's Weekly et al, 36;

BOOKS:
Capricornia, 23, 24, 28, 35, 36, 37, 38, 39, 40, 41, 42, *44-46*, 67, 70, 76, 77, 89, 90, 95, 97, 100, 101, 107, 108, 109, 110, 113, 132-33
Disturbing Element, 23, 24, 26, 28, 31, 33, 34, 48, 56, 77, 135n2, 136n7
Larger Than Life 36, 76, *97-108*
"A.T.C. Barragoola", 105
"An Eagle Called Ned Kelly", 106, 107
"Come On Murri", 99, 103
"Day of Shame", 112

147

"Femme Fatale", 107
"Kaiijeck the Songman", 105, 108
"Keeping the Peace", 100, 101-102
"Last Toss", 108
"Look Into My Eyes!'", 99, 102, 107
"Marrying Money", 101, 107-108
"Mercy Flight", 101-102, 105, 108
"Michaelos Is a Miser!'", 107
"Moonshine", 101, 103
"Once a Policeman," 1
"Rise And Fall of Jeremiah Stacey",
  100, 102, 103, 107
"Rocky The Rig.", 99, 100, 102,
  103, 107
"Sequel To A Song", 100, 104-105,
  108
"The Best Laid Plans", 102, 103
"The Flying Fat Boy", 105, 106
"Miss Tanaka", 107
Poor Fellow My Country, 24, 29, 35,
  40, 42, 43, 51, 54, 56, 72, 77, 105,
  109-32
Seven Emus, 41, 42, *67-76*, 89, 100,
  101, 110
Soldier's Women, 41, 42, 67, *77-96*,
  99, 100, 110-11, 113, 116, 133,
  135n10

ESSAYS AND OCCASIONAL ARTICLES:
"Autobiographette", 23-24, 26
"A Town Like Elliot", 74, 138n14
"Herbert's Retort To Stephenson",
  136n30
"How Capricornia Was Made",
  136n27
"I Sinned Against Syntax", 40, 67
  136n13, 137n39
"I, The Little Widow And The
  World", 27, 40
"My Thousandth Death", 25, 136n6
"The Signing Of The Peace Treaty",
  137n40
"The Writing of Capricornia", 136n26

UNPUBLISHED OR ABANDONED WORKS:
Black Velvet, 35, 37
*Sacred to the Memory Of the Scrub
  Bull*, 40
The King And The Kurrawaddi, 40
"The Speaking Fish", 27

Hergenhan, Laurie (Dr.), 42, 54, 135n14,
  137n26
Heseltine, Harry (Dr.), 42, 65, 71, 78,
  79, 108, 137n38, 137n29, 140n17; *Xavier Herbert*, 42, 56
Hetherington, John, 135n8
Hope, A.D., 59, 135n3
Hughes, W., 120, 125
Huxley, Aldous, 36

Jonathan Cape, 36, 37

Kiernan, Brian, 65, 135n11, 138n47
Kynaston, Edward, 135n12

Lawrence, D.H., 36, 98; *Lady Chatterley's Lover*, 36
Lawson, Henry, 67
Lindsay, Jack, 36
Lindsay, Norman, 36, 38
London Aphrodite, 36

MacArthur, Douglas, 120
Mandrake Press, 36
Maupassant, Guy de, 98
Maurice, Furnley, 135n5, 137n1
Meanjin, 27, 136n13, 136n14, 136n32
Menzies, Robert, 120
Miles, W.J., 38
Moby Dick, 47
Morrisby, Camden, 35, 36, 135n1
McCullough, Colleen: *The Thorn Birds*,
  46
McRae, Hugh, 36

O'Flaherty, Liam, 36
Overland, 135n12

Penton, Brian, 36; *Landtakers*, 46
Powers, T.F., 36
Publicist, The, 23, 38, 67, 135n1, 136n33

Quadrant, 136n6

The Rape of the Lock, 82
Reid, Ian, 136n32
Robertson, Jillian, 135n2
Rolfe, Patricia, 35, 37, 135n9
Ruhen, Olaf, 37

Index 149